BRAVE NEW
WORKSHOP

Wishing you laughter
and insight. Enjoy!

Rob Hubbard

BRAVE NEW WORKSHOP

PROMISCUOUS
HOSTILITY AND
LAUGHS IN THE
LAND OF LOONS

ROB HUBBARD

Foreword by Al Franken

THE
History
PRESS

Published by The History Press
Charleston, SC
www.historypress.net

Copyright © 2015 by Rob Hubbard
All rights reserved

All images courtesy of Brave New Workshop except where indicated.

First published 2015

Manufactured in the United States

ISBN 978.1.62619.686.5

Library of Congress Control Number: 2015943179

*For Sosan Theresa Flynn and Seamus Hubbard Flynn,
who bring laughter into my life every day and without whose love and support
this book would not have been possible.*

CONTENTS

CONTENTS

FOREWORD

Tom Davis and I were in high school when we discovered Dudley Riggs'
Brave New Workshop. This was in 1968 or maybe 1969, my senior
year. I didn't take notes back then.

We had been doing some comedy of our own in school. Adults at schools
actually encourage you to get on a stage. So when young people who are still
in school ask me how to get started in comedy, I usually ask them whether
they're doing comedy. If they're not, I tell them, "You're in school! They
want you to get on the stage at school. After you leave school, no one wants
you to get up on a stage."

When we went to our first show at the Workshop, we saw actual adults on
the stage doing what we wanted to do—make audiences laugh. After the show,
we stayed for the improv set. We'd never seen anything like it—the cast making
stuff up on their feet from audience suggestions. It was a bit hit or miss, but that
made it even more hilarious—and exhilarating—when they scored.

Tom and I started to be regulars—not regular customers, exactly. The
improv sets were free, so we'd arrive at the end of the regular sketch show
and stay through the entire improv session, laughing and marveling at how
consistently funny they were. We began to notice some technique. If one of
the actors "discovered" an object or a place or a situation during a scene, all
of the other players immediately embraced it. In improv terms, this is known
as "saying yes."

Later, we'd learn that they were using techniques similar to those developed
by Del Close and others at Second City in Chicago. We were watching a

Brave New Workshop alumni Al Franken and Tom Davis in a 1972 publicity shot for their comedy act. Three years later, they were hired as writers and performers for the first incarnation of NBC's *Saturday Night Live*, but they still returned to perform at Dudley Riggs' ETC.

school of comedy in its relative infancy that would produce the likes of John Belushi, Dan Aykroyd, Jane Curtin and Bill Murray through Will Ferrell, Tina Fey, Amy Poehler and on and on.

The theater was small. Sometimes, by the end of the improv set, there'd be ten or fifteen audience members left. So the performers began to notice

Tom and me as well, and we got up the nerve to talk to them. They were all just a few years older than us. I'd call them kids now.

We met Dudley Riggs, impresario and former vaudevillian and circus performer—certainly no kid. To two teenagers from suburban Minneapolis, this was exotic—kind of a cross between meeting Lorne Michaels (if Lorne Michaels had been Lorne Michaels then) and Professor Marvel, the kind-hearted traveling con man from *The Wizard of Oz*.

Dudley was friendly and suggested we come to an open stage night and do ten minutes, so we did.

We led off with a local newscast on the night of the first day of World War III. "Tragedy! Death! Catastrophe! Highlights on tonight's news, after this message…The stock market closed today—for good. And now with the sports, Barney Johnson…Temperatures up to ten thousand degrees in the Twin Cities today."

We got solid laughs, and Dudley told us he "saw sparks." By the summer, we were doing one show a week at the Workshop. My mom decided we should be billed as Franken and Davis because I was a year older than Tom. Also, we got paid! Tom and I were professional comedians!

At the end of the summer, I went off to college and Tom back to high school for his senior year. Throughout the next four years, Dudley's became a touchstone for Franken and Davis. During the summers, we did shows at the Hennepin Avenue theater while the main cast performed at the new, larger Washington Avenue theater near the University of Minnesota.

Tom dropped out of college after his sophomore year and became a Brave New Workshop cast member. Tom was wonderful and especially hilarious in the improv sets. I've always regretted not having that training. But one half of Franken and Davis did, and it would play a big role in the material we created, both for ourselves and then later on *Saturday Night Live* (*SNL*).

During my summer vacations from college, Dudley would give us the Hennepin Avenue theater for our evolving two-man show. Again, we got paid, augmenting income from my day job at my suburb's street department. Starting in the early morning, I'd spend my time in the hot sun, sitting on a huge industrial mower, cutting grass and weeds on city property. At night, I was entertaining folks at a theater that didn't serve liquor. They were polite, open-minded, responsive Minnesotans. It was a beautiful summer in almost every way.

Unfortunately, I sometimes get migraines. And, as the summer wore on, the hours started wearing on my noggin. One night, I came to the theater with a horrific migraine throbbing from a point behind my right eye. Now,

11

there is nothing worse for a throbbing migraine than stage lights. So right before the show, I told Tom that he should be prepared to kill time if I had to go backstage to throw up. Fortunately, he had been working on a couple monologues and covered for me whenever I'd run backstage and hurl into a strategically placed wastebasket.

As he often did, Dudley had come in that night to see how we were progressing. Being the showman he is, Dudley immediately saw what was going on and stayed to the end to compliment us and dispense some of his legendary showbiz wisdom. As I lay on a backstage couch, face down in a pillow, Dudley told us a hard and fast rule of live entertainment: if a performer throws up onstage, the audience leaves.

Between my junior and senior years in college, Tom and I hitchhiked from Minneapolis to Los Angeles to check out the comedy scene there. That's right; we hitchhiked. It was 1972, a more innocent time in America, and we were especially innocent and stupid.

But we got safely to Hollywood and stayed at Pat Proft's small apartment. Pat was one of our favorite cast members from the Workshop and had moved to L.A. to do stand-up at the Comedy Store, then the club in Hollywood for aspiring stand-ups. Pat was a wonderfully gifted performer, but you don't know him because his back went out in a very serious way just as he was getting noticed. You do know his work, however. Pat would go on to write or co-write movies like the *Police Academy*, *Naked Gun* and *Hot Shots* series.

Not only did Pat provide a couple couches for us to crash on, but he also got us a spot to do a twenty-minute set at the Comedy Store. We killed and instantly elevated our status in the comedy world to comedians who could show up at the Comedy Store and get up onstage to perform for free. We felt pretty damn good about ourselves.

Tom went back to Dudley's, and I went back to my senior year in college. In the spring, Tom came east to stay in my dorm room. On weekends, we'd drive down to New York in a beat-up '62 Buick LeSabre that my uncle Erwin had given me to play the Improv, a comedy club near Times Square—the East Coast Comedy Store. We were performing with comics like Jay Leno, Freddie Prinze, Jimmy Walker and Andy Kaufman.

We still were performing for free. At the time, there was no circuit of comedy clubs named Zanies, Chuckles or the Punch Line (across the street from the Set Up), so these were lean times for young stand-ups. The Workshop was still the only place that had paid us.

After I graduated from college in June 1973, Tom and I and my college sweetheart—now my wife of forty years and the mother of my children,

Franni—loaded up the Buick and headed to Los Angeles. We did more Comedy Store performances, some paid gigs at colleges in the Midwest and at a club in Pasadena, plus a stint as Santa Claus and Winnie the Pooh at the Sears in North Hollywood. (Tom and I switched every few hours because, for some reason, kids just love to shove Winnie.)

Then, on a Friday afternoon in July 1975, we got a call from our agent who had sent our writing sample to guy named Lorne Michaels. I still remember the packet we sent. It was just fourteen pages long and included a commercial parody, a sketch, a short film and a news broadcast on the night of the first day of World War III—the piece we first performed at Dudley's. I told Tom that any show that hired us based on our submission would be a giant hit. Youthful arrogance is correct every once in a while.

After the first season of *SNL*, Tom and I made a triumphant return to the Brave New Workshop for a sold-out, two-week run. Franken and Davis returned to where we had started as conquering heroes. Well, as local boys who were part of a new cultural phenomenon.

UNITED STATES SENATORS OFTEN rise to speak on the floor when a prominent person from their state passes. Tom died of cancer in July 2012, just before his sixtieth birthday. Here's some of what I said:

Tom created laughter. The obituaries cited some of Tom's body of work. He and Dan Aykroyd created the Coneheads. Tom was the key collaborator with Bill Murray on Nick the Lounge Singer.

This started an outpouring of blogging on the Internet, people writing about Tom and the laughs he brought them. I was happy to see him get his due. People called him an original. He was. They called him a brilliant comedian. He was.

Tom was an improvisational genius. The first public stage we performed on was at Dudley Riggs' Brave New Workshop. Dudley's was essentially the Minneapolis version of Second City, based on the same improvisational techniques. Tom and I did stand-up at Dudley's, not improv. But while I went off to college, Tom joined the cast at Dudley's, and when I came back, I saw that he had mastered improv and mastered it hilariously.

As a writing team, Tom and I brought different strengths to our craft. Sometimes we'd get stuck, and Tom would "find" an object. In the third year of *SNL*, Tom and I saw Julia Child cut herself while doing a cooking segment on *The Today Show*, I think it was. So we wrote a sketch, which Danny performed brilliantly, that is now known as "Julia Child Bleeding to Death."

When Tom and I were writing it, we couldn't find an ending to the piece, and Tom "found" an object—the phone. The phone hanging on the wall of Julia Child's cooking set. That's something improv artists do when they're on the stage. They find objects to work with.

So Danny as Julia Child was spurting blood, and she was trying everything, explaining how to make a tourniquet out of a chicken bone and a dishtowel or how to use the chicken liver as a natural coagulant. Nothing was working, and she was losing blood. So in desperation, she saw the phone on the wall, turned to it and said, "Always have the emergency number written down on the phone. Oh, it isn't!" But she grabbed it, saying, "It's 9-1-1!" and punched the numbers. She discovered "It's a prop phone" and threw it down in disgust and resignation. She started getting woozy and then rambled about eating chopped chicken liver on crackers as a child and finally collapsed. She was about to die and said one more "Save the liver."

I had the strong feeling that nothing quite like this had been discussed before on the Senate floor. Then again, no other senator had started his career with his high school buddy at a small satirical improv theater.

AL FRANKEN

Al Franken and Tom Davis reunited at a 2008 celebration of the fiftieth anniversary of Dudley Riggs opening the original Café Espresso.

ACKNOWLEDGEMENTS

The author wishes to thank all of those who were so generous with their time, stories and reflections on their experiences at the Brave New Workshop. First and foremost, my gratitude to Dudley Riggs, as well as to Al Franken, Richard Guindon, Dan Sullivan, Vince Williams, Pat Proft, Tom Sherohman and his brothers, Michael Anthony, Anita Anderson O'Sullivan, Michael McManus, Scott Pollock, Ann Ryerson, John Remington, Nancy Steen, Mark Keller, Louie Anderson, Susan Fuller, Scott Novotny, Peggy Knapp, Peter Tolan, Jeff Cesario, Sue Scott, Beth Gilleland, Dane Stauffer, Steve Rentfrow, Greg Triggs, Butch Roy, Peter Guertin, Caleb McEwen, Josh Eakright, Pauline Boss and the family of Irv Letofsky, who left behind a treasure trove of scripts and a marvelous memoir about the early days of the Brave New Workshop called *Promiscuous Comedy*. Special thanks to Erin Farmer, Jenni Lilledahl and John Sweeney for all of their time and assistance in the archaeological excavations necessary to bring this book to life. And thanks to my editor, Greg Dumais, and The History Press for the opportunity to tell this story.

The exterior of Brave New Workshop's longtime home at 2605 South Hennepin Avenue in Minneapolis, pictured in 2007 while it was presenting *Pluto; and Other Lies My Teacher Told Me*.

1

BRICKS THROUGH THE WINDOWS, NAZIS IN THE BASEMENT; OR, FAREWELL 2605

S tep right up!

   Feast your eyes and ears on the wonder that is the Brave New Workshop. Swing open the door on this red, white and blue Minneapolis storefront bedecked in the Stars and Stripes of our native land. Keep to your left, please, and advance to the ticket windows, which you'll find peering out from the side of a colorfully adorned circus train car. Gird your loins, awaken your conscience and stretch out your cerebellum, for you are about to avail yourself of the wonder that is the Brave New Workshop, one of the world's great comedic landmarks.

   It is here, my fine friends, that the history of American comedy was jolted with a seismic shift back in the 1960s, producing cultural temblors ever since. A place where laughter became a tool of the counterculture, where mockery of the powerful became a nightly occurrence, where all sides got it from all sides.

   Step into this hothouse, which has fertilized and nurtured comedic skills for over half a century, bringing to bloom the careers of those who helped shape your beloved *Saturday Night Live*, the unapologetically silly *Naked Gun* movies and *A Prairie Home Companion* and has been unleashing actors, screenwriters, comedians, playwrights and even a U.S. senator on the unsuspecting public with ferocious regularity.

   You have come on an auspicious evening, for tonight we say farewell to this humble storefront, which has been the principal home for this incubator of insight, this lyceum of laughter for forty-nine years. Not goodbye to Brave New Workshop, oh no. Its satirical heart pumps more loudly than ever; its accounts are in unprecedented health; its dedication is undimmed. In fact, it outgrew these humble environs a few years ago and still lies on the same thoroughfare that has hosted this intrepid troupe since 1961, Minneapolis's Hennepin Avenue. But it is downtown now, taking its place among the restaurants, bars and hotels at the nexus of this Midwestern metropolis, appropriately ensconced among a cluster of beautifully restored historic theaters.

And that's appropriate for a theater company as historic as the Brave New Workshop. Accept as evidence the testimony of the many gathered on this night at 2605 South Hennepin Avenue in Minneapolis's Uptown neighborhood. Listen to those who take the stage and sing its praises, recounting marvelous memories and absurd adventures. It is September 17, 2014, and the lease is up. Brave New Workshop will no longer have a presence in this funky little venue to which it first moved in November 1965. Tears will be shed and stories shared at this strange little theater space with an onstage elevator shaft and bar, revolving panels, a dark and precipitous backstage staircase and virtually nowhere to change costumes.

Among those gathered is the company's now-eighty-something patriarch and longtime leader, Dudley Riggs, a former circus clown and aerialist who thought that comedy might be a good way to get people into the coffeehouse that held what he believed to be America's first espresso machine west of Chicago. The room overflows with his partners in parody, for present are creators of comedy from each decade in the Brave New Workshop's history.

The emcee for this evening's program is the dashing, *GQ* cover–friendly Caleb McEwen, who has been the company's artistic director for twelve years. It is his caricature that adorns the whiteboard at the bottom of the narrow staircase to the dressing rooms, a wry smile on its lips and the words, "Perfect. Yes!" emerging from them. ("Yes" is also written in lipstick on a nearby makeup mirror, giving any visitor the sense that this is an affirming environment.)

Alumni ascend to the stage to talk about building this space, meeting their spouses here—even though a female friend of McEwen's said before his first visit that "going out with a Brave New Workshop guy takes a lot of energy"—embracing the camaraderie and principles of improvisation, never negating and always adding on with a "Yes, and…"

Finally, Riggs takes the stage for a dialogue with company co-owner John Sweeney, regaling the audience with tales of sharing the space with a Nazi paraphernalia peddler; hiding a toilet seat that he felt was too often used as a cheap-laugh-producing *deus ex machina* for sketches going nowhere; the

The circus wagon ticket windows at 2605 South Hennepin Avenue, a reminder of founder Dudley Riggs's history as an aerialist and clown.

Vietnam era, when draft cards were burned onstage, weddings performed to secure draft deferments, and bricks came through the windows late at night.

The most touching speech comes from a current company member, Lauren Anderson, the garrulous blonde who's been one of the staples and signature performers of Brave New Workshop casts since early this century. She speaks of the classes she teaches; of how a high school student told her that she wanted to change gender and wished to tell Anderson first because "this is the safest place I know"; and of an older student diagnosed with cancer who kept coming to class because "improv helps me fight." As for her experience creating and performing shows at Brave New Workshop, Anderson said, "It always felt more like a pirate ship than a theater."

This is the story of that ship's journey.

Company founder Dudley Riggs at the Italian espresso machine that gave Café Espresso its name, pictured in 1958, the year the café opened at 18 University Avenue Northeast, Minneapolis. *Courtesy of the* Star Tribune.

2

A CAFFEINE-ASSISTED AWAKENING;
OR, SOMETHING ON SUNDAYS

Dullsville, Daddy-o. That's what Minneapolis was to many of those who came of age in the twilight of the Eisenhower era. Maybe jazz, folk and rock 'n' roll, adventurous art and inventive theater were happening in places like New York City or a day's drive down U.S. 12 in Chicago, but not in Minneapolis.

But what would you expect from a city that was built around milling flour? Plain white flour. A place where folks with names like Washburn, Crosby and Pillsbury got rich by using the Mississippi River's restless current to grind up the grain that had rolled in by rail from the sprawling plains to the west.

That industry had been dying for decades by the 1960s, and students at the University of Minnesota and the area's many private colleges were growing weary of the lack of excitement in a town now known for breakfast cereals and banking. And if there's one thing more boring than flour, it's banking.

What this city needed was a wake-up call, and maybe that's why—in a kind of "let it begin with me" move—folks in their teens and twenties started hanging around in coffeehouses. Not coffee shops—the look-alike, long-countered linoleum places where wing-tipped businessmen tossed their ties over their shoulders and java down their throats before running off to the next meeting. No, we're talking about slow-paced sanctuaries where candles and conversation were the norm, where talk of philosophy, politics and literature filled the air. A place like the Jazz Lab that Richard

Guindon ran on St. Paul's Payne Avenue. It was a bit off the beaten path on the city's East Side, but it still drew a crowd that came for coffee complemented by what may have been the Twin Cities' only jukebox that played modern jazz. The music was occasionally live, too, but strictly jazz, even if folkies like Bob Dylan—while living in the Twin Cities in 1959 and '60—showed up and asked to play for tips. At least that's what Guindon's partner, Perry Cucchiarella, maintained for years, adding that he told Dylan to take a hike.

One person who had heard about the Jazz Lab was an ex–circus performer who had recently moved to the Twin Cities. His name was Dudley Riggs.

"It was a winter night," Guindon recalled in a relaxed, grandfatherly voice with sandpaper edges. "And he was on a god-damned bicycle. And here's this Ichabod Crane coming through the door. Dudley was always very thin. He introduced himself, an ex–circus performer, et cetera, et cetera. He was very fun. I guess he'd just heard of the place. And there wasn't much open."

Perhaps because it kept late hours—"We'd open nine or ten at night and close whenever the last people left; or if they didn't want to leave, I'd ask them to close up, if I knew them," Guindon said—it was also an after-work hangout for journalists done putting the morning paper together. One of them was Irv Letofsky, an editor with the *St. Paul Pioneer Press*.

It was the late 1950s, and St. Paul was just as lifeless as its neighbor to the west, Minneapolis.

"There was nothing open at night," Guindon recalled. "There were no pizza places, there was no anything. There were some breakfast shops in St. Paul. It was really quite dead at night. There wasn't a lot of shopping in the evening. You'd go through a neighborhood with stores and drugstores and, after six or seven at night, your whole neighborhood would be black."

Having journalists in the joint led Guindon to ask how they could get some publicity for their place.

"Irv gave us step-by-step 'here's what you can do.' A wide variety of things—very common sense. But I was very impressed by his step-by-step. He knew exactly what he was talking about. He was a new friend, and I liked him. He had a nice, dry wit."

It wasn't long before Riggs opened his own coffeehouse near the University of Minnesota in Minneapolis, a converted garage at 18 University Avenue Northeast that he called Café Espresso. It was 1958, and Riggs established a niche: if the young people of Minneapolis wanted a wakeup call, he would provide it with the espresso machine he had purchased in Italy while on tour with a circus. It was so foreign to local licensing authorities that they forced Riggs to get training as a boiler operator. But Café Espresso became popular enough to inspire an expansion to a larger space around the corner at 207 East Hennepin Avenue. Well, that makes it sound as if it was Riggs's idea. Actually, he was evicted.

And larger is a relative term. It was a long, narrow room with a stage at the far end. Actually, there were two stages of uneven heights, one smaller than the other. Riggs hired Guindon as what would nowadays be called a barista. It wasn't long before Riggs started pondering out loud how his little coffeehouse could get the attention of the local papers. Guindon said, "You ought to talk to my friend."

That friend was Irv Letofsky. In the late spring of 1961, he was invited to Café Espresso for a confab about drumming up press coverage.

"Irv had just come from a comedy thing that the press used to do, *The Gridiron Show*," Guindon recalled. "He had just done that the week before, and he was really quite besotted by it. Keep in mind that there were a lot of new comics, a great deal of energy in the comedy world. Second City, et cetera, et cetera. And he said: Why don't we do something like…I don't know if he used the words 'Second City,' but he wanted to do little playlets."

Riggs had been involved in theatrical pursuits ever since he left the circus act in which he had been raised and flung about. A variety show troupe that he'd assembled in New York concluded its tour in Minneapolis, so he decided to settle down for a little while and go to school.

While attending the University of Minnesota, he opened the coffeehouse and started hosting performers. He encouraged improvisation, reviving the name and structure of a New York group he had led called "Instant Theater." Over time, other groups emerged within the space, like the John Birch Society Players. But he was looking for something to get crowds in on slow Sunday nights. When they met, Letofsky talked about *The Gridiron Show*.

"*The Gridiron Show* worked a little like the roasts they do on television," Riggs said in something like a baritone version of the voice of mid-twentieth-century comedian Ed Wynn. "One of the scribes would say, 'I've got this song about [cannibalistic mass murderer] Ed Gein.' Something he would sing at a barroom party. It would have a giggle to it and would be added to *The Gridiron Show*."

Riggs was intrigued with the idea of building off that concept but wanted to set some ground rules.

"I said that, if we're going to have a meeting about this, everyone should come with some ideas."

Letofsky asked a young colleague at the *Pioneer Press*, Dan Sullivan, to be part of the process.

"We had a meeting at someone's house in Minneapolis," Sullivan recalled in the measured tone of a tenured college professor, "and decided that, if we could come up with one hundred ideas—stuff that was funny enough to merit some sort of a sketch or at least a wisecrack in the show—then we would do it."

So they gathered at closing time at Café Espresso on June 15, 1961. Present at the meeting were Riggs, Guindon, Letofsky, Sullivan and a playwright named John Lewin.

"I was secretary," Sullivan said, "so I compiled the list and kept it…Things like: Caroline Kennedy in the Oval Office while [John F.] Kennedy's on the phone with Khrushchev. Mostly current events stuff.

"So we started, and Irv's idea was that we would have two companies. We would call ours the 'Brave New Workshop'," inspired by Aldous Huxley's novel *Brave New World*, "and John Lewin would captain another company that would perform every other Sunday."

The notepad that launched Brave New Workshop, on which Dan Sullivan scrawled down the one hundred ideas for comedy sketches that he, Richard Guindon, Irv Letofsky, John Lewin and Dudley Riggs brainstormed through the night on June 15, 1961.

· Dr. Wilson as
principle of school
— Kid is flunking
graduate school, sez
Mother, why?

literary quarterly
popular like
Playboy

the new Philistine
hates Bermudas

Peace corps? Shrinking
heads — how do you
do that?
    I've come to show you
how to plow your
land.
    It's an oil tank.
— That arm looks bad.
    I'd help
you w my snake
bit kit but we're not
supposed to help
you.

Psychiatrist — "Fuck
'em!" + patient who
knows all the jargon
— what
history really
happened?

whatever happened
to the great
imposter? He's
a matter superior.
"I'll take a shower
later — you guys
go ahead."

Helen Keller
will the real
Helen Keller
stand up?
(photo facing
wall)

"the untouchables"
Norman
Mailer

This page and next two: Pages of the notepad full of one hundred ideas.

25

Ancel Keys — "and you never outgrow your need for milk."

Gusskind — small talk "good coffee" "do you take a bus" "who's going to ride w me" the man who brought back the art of conversation

Ingmar Bergman "the god-man image facing —" "gee, I meant to see that" See ae-run of National Velvet "yeah, Elizabeth Taylor nice little body for 14-year — oh, are we still on?"

Dave Beck as Mister Kleen

Sacco-Venzetti Rosenbergs

GE price fixing labor at Cape Canaveral

Noxzema Sandra Dee

Ed Gein

Pasternak, Bernstein Alexander King B. Russell — cheeks other cheek

Thelonius Monk on baseball

"... and that boy was —"

Glenn Miller "no it goes like this ..."

"I was still using the improv blackboard," Riggs recalled, "and we put things down on that until two or three in the morning. John Lewin filtered through the ideas and came back with a fully written script. And so his production company, his efforts, were kind of in competition with Brave New Workshop."

The material was as lowbrow as a Helen Keller joke (never used) and as highbrow as Russian novelist Boris Pasternak, but the group did indeed come up with one hundred ideas. From there, Lewin and Letofsky cobbled together separate scripts. The plan was for the Brave New Workshop and Lewin's company, Second Finger, to alternate Sunday nights. But the two companies debuted by banding together for one long show on Wednesday, June 28, 1961, taking the stage to "Happy Days Are Here Again."

Letofsky recalled in his 2007 memoir *Promiscuous Comedy*: "Opening night was happy, for sure, if chaotic. We hadn't thought much about lengths of the bits and the two companies ran well beyond three hours. The best thing was a series of beatnik poets as rendered by John. Hysterical. But despite a lot of laughs, it was a sweaty evening."

However, Minneapolis had begun its metamorphosis from dullsville to a happening town. Well, happening on Hennepin, anyway. The Brave New Workshop was born.

Café Espresso and its East Hennepin neighbors are pictured in 1963. Surdyk's has since moved to a larger space a block east and remains among the Twin Cities area's most popular liquor stores. *Collection of Keith Fountain.*

3

BETWEEN THE BLACKOUTS;
OR, A REVOLUTION IN SUEDE
JACKETS AND MGs

*N*ew Ideas, 1961.
That was the title of the first revue, although Riggs was reluctant.

I felt: Oh boy, I'm hesitant to put this banner up, because I thought they'd say: "Who the hell are you to talk about new ideas?" But, oddly enough, we got some business.

It was a very quiet city when it started, and we developed our following because we were a little bit off. Enough off the beaten path to be doing something that other people weren't. We weren't creating Chekhov or Shakespeare, but some creative juices were running. For a time, it was a colloquy of newspaper people. When we had that newspaper strike, it came at a time when they had a little more time. A lot of breakthroughs.

It certainly was a breakthrough for Richard Guindon.
"The culture was changing," he said.

Just as your father's jokes don't necessarily work for you... We were seeing this new stuff coming on and wanted to be part of it. We were seeing our first European films; we never saw those, because Hollywood kept them out of our market. So it was a time of change, and you're young and you're feeling that energy and excitement that comes with that.

Everyone was wearing Oxford Club shirts and suede jackets. Jazz was just making its move. There were a few sports cars in the Twin Cities, so few that they would honk at each other as they passed. Like MGs. Dudley naturally had one of them. With the canvas top and the plastic windows. It was a whole tsunami of cultural change. It predated things like the hippies by quite a bit.

And comedy was part of the change.

Guindon said, "What we used to do is play Lenny Bruce or Nichols and May albums for dates and, if they didn't get it, this was a Rorschach test for your date."

Brave New Workshop was ready to ride this cultural wave. But first, more people needed to get involved.

"We posted something at the coffee shop and at the university theater, until it was taken down," Riggs said.

Something saying that we were interested in actors, writers and musicians. In that sense, we were doing it like casting a play. Once people knew that their idea could actually find an audience—that warmed things considerably. Now, we have that kind of creative energy blooming all over town, but, at that point, it was kind of forbidden stuff. Espresso was already suspect. And someone would call up and say: "I don't know if I want my daughter at a rehearsal at your place at 1:30 in the morning" or whatever the fear would be. So it took a while to find people with enough freedom and enough courage to go out on stage without a script.

The early years, I don't think we ever had an occasion when someone said: You absolutely cannot do that. So we thought, "Why not?"

Vince Williams was an early member of the troupe.

"If memory serves, I think I saw a blurb in the *Minneapolis Tribune*," he recalled.

In that early planning meeting I attended, I had the impression this would be generally political satire, with some sort of "cultural" sections tossed in. In some of those early shows and rehearsals, I dreamed up the idea of interspersing "blackouts" with "bits." The former being skits with a punch line ending and the "bits" being very short, such as one person on stage in a spotlight saying, "Now here's a word for hemorrhoid sufferers: DON'T SIT DOWN!" Blackout!

"The crowds were very skimpy sometimes," Dan Sullivan recalled.

Sometimes they were good. But it was so much fun to do. I just thought, "It's ridiculous, but let's just keep on doing it." We never thought about money. It was just kind of a lark. I was single. There was no particular design. Any one of us could have quit, and no one wanted to quit. Nothing was really expected or demanded of us, just to have fun in our sandbox. And I always thought that we owed Dudley fealty for giving us a place, a stage to try our stuff.

Sometimes the comedy was inspired by stories ripped from the next day's headlines.

"Dudley was fun to work with," Sullivan said. "He would do a monologue that he would pretty much make up on the spot, going up there with the early edition of the next day's *Tribune*. He would read things on page one and then make up something. He was good, and I think would be still if he were interested in doing that."

"That may have just been a natural transition from the vaudeville act, using the paper," Riggs said.

It seemed that it was also a way to explain how we arrived at what we were about to present. If the show had a real subject, we'd tack on a few things about that. So I got in the habit of those at the opening or sometimes doing a second-act opening. That kind of went away when we lost half of the newspapers. Once they no longer provided a blue streak [an early edition], I wasn't able to provide tomorrow's news tonight. If everybody's already read the paper—or now, has heard the news—it doesn't make that gig work.

The shows had a thrown-together feel, especially for the performers.

"We would all be backstage, fumbling around," Sullivan said. "Dudley was the one, for some reason, who would determine what the order of the sketches would be. It seems to me he would write them on a shirt cardboard that he would put up in the kitchen in the café. It would always go up pretty late and would always be a surprise."

But Riggs would indeed emerge from his disheveled lair of an office with the plan for the evening. That office was so messy that many found it frightening to visit. Richard Guindon recalled, "I used to say that if ever Dudley was missing and people looked for him in his office, they would assume not only that he had been kidnapped, but that he had put up a hell of a fight."

Riggs said, "There is a point in time when someone needs to say this works and this doesn't. I used to have the job of nudging the show back and forth. If the middle of the road would start veering toward the left, I'd start

The humble exterior of Café Espresso at 207 East Hennepin Avenue in 1963, when it had become a destination nightspot for comedy in Minneapolis.

nudging to the middle, so we wouldn't be preaching to the liberal choir. So I think, in a way, I was the conscience of trying to maintain something."

Guindon said, "Everyone was wondering: Could we really sustain this? The problem was that Minneapolis wasn't fraught with corruption and things that we were going to do wonderful political material about. You didn't have material readily available."

But he credits Letofsky with making it work.

"I was a gag writer of sorts, but Irv was the facilitator," Guindon said. "Irv would write everything down; it was his memory that kept it all together. He was the scribe, but he was also the adult in the group."

Sullivan describes Letofsky similarly:

> Irv was the grownup among us, the one who insisted that we'd better get our copy in. He was always the director, and did a lot of the writing. If I wrote a piece and he liked it, then we'd do it. He would write stuff, and I would make suggestions. It was very informal. It was mainly the two of us and Dick Guindon early on.
>
> Granted, Irv and I would be doing some of the writing while we were at the office at the Pioneer Press. The typewriters were there, so...It was

very casual at the time. It was a good newspaper, a great newspaper to start out on. The deadlines weren't too onerous. And that's what we would do in our free time. It was just a pleasure.

Soon the cadre of writers and performers expanded. Riggs recalled:

At one point in 1961, I think we had about forty-eight different people writing, one of whom was Gary Keillor [now known as Garrison Keillor, author and host of the public radio variety show *A Prairie Home Companion*]. *So* New Ideas, 1961 *marked the beginning of primarily scripted material. The improvisation troupe, which was still running, lost its momentum.*

"Dudley Riggs is too kind in remembering me writing sketches for the Workshop," Garrison Keillor said. "I did write them, but the Workshop turned them down, as they should have done. Irv Letofsky wrote for them, and Dan Sullivan. But I did not, alas."

Sullivan said:

The difference between the Workshop then and the Workshop now is it was basically the writers were giving the actors things to do. Now the actors could improve upon them, but the actors were not particularly into improv. They were just hungry to do stuff. They were ambitious actors. There were never any big fights about, "No, you're an actor; you can't do that." We seemed to have done this in real harmony, but I think it was because it really didn't matter. It was just fun.

Guindon said that Sullivan's musicianship contributed to the success of the early revues.

Dan's piano made more skits work than anything else because we couldn't go dark for blackouts. So we'd come up to the end and, theoretically, in comedy, you want to end with the strongest joke. And then you go BOOM, and, hopefully, there's some laughter there. What started happening was we started to think: what's funny here isn't the last thing, it's the concept. So the premise became the joke, and that made it harder to finish the skit because you didn't have a big laugh. So what would happen is that we'd go dark, as it were, but—if it wasn't at night or we were running in summer when the daylight is still there—the people are still onstage when the lights go down. But Dan would be there at the piano, playing them off.

Sullivan said, "My observation is that, to me, this was a casual kind of hobby thing that I did to do fun things with my friends and have a gang to hang around with."

A kind of iconoclasm was taking hold in American culture. Comedy was getting hipper and more irreverent, and Brave New Workshop was becoming part of that.

Dick Guindon said:

> *I remember Irv inviting me along when he interviewed Lenny Bruce. We spent a great deal of time talking to him. There was a whole new group of comics. Lenny was a little more cutting edge than the others. But up until then, comics were more guys out of the Borscht Belt, always in immaculate suits. And then along came people like Mort Sahl and Nichols and May, who were so intellectual, and Second City, the whole wave of not just comedy, but eggheadedness became popular—intellectualism, Ivy League looks.*

Richard Guindon's painted sign on the side of the building that housed Café Espresso on East Hennepin Avenue in Minneapolis, pictured in 1962. *Collection of Keith Fountain.*

I remember Lenny talking about the Twin Cities at the time and saying that there aren't any boondocks anymore. People are starting to get hip all over the country. It used to be that it was only New York, L.A. and San Francisco. And I didn't quite agree with him. I thought, "No, we're still in the boondocks out here."

Dudley Riggs displays that he still has his aerialist acumen on Café Espresso's opening night in 1958.

4

A BIT ABOUT DUDLEY;
OR, FOR WHOM THE BOW TIES

So who is this Dudley Riggs character anyway? Well, he certainly is a character, so much so that even some who have ended up working at Brave New Workshop assumed before arriving that he was some fictional icon, like Paul Bunyan or the Hamm's Bear. They thought that the jowly, smiling caricature that appeared on the theater's signs and dispatches was of someone created for advertising purposes, with the perfect name to match.

But no, Dudley is very much a man. A man who, like most, started out as a child. But unlike most in that your average four-year-old doesn't ride in a wagon being pulled by a polar bear. That's what happens when you're born into the circus, as Riggs was. His parents were aerialists, barnstorming about the United States and Europe in the company of a variety of clowns, lion tamers and knife throwers. Born into the Great Depression in 1932, Riggs was raised by a couple who trusted each other with their lives every night, being trapeze artists who had the potential to accelerate household spats to a lethal level but never did.

Dudley earned his keep as part of the act, balancing himself upside down atop his father's head while pitching the show to passing pedestrians, then tumbling around the big top and, eventually, ascending rope ladders for more demanding derring-do. It was a life of trains and tents, sawdust and hay and fellow performers schooling young Dudley as de facto tutors. He flew, he fell, he suffered injuries and he was a clown while recovering.

When winter approached, a time when other circus performers rested, young Dudley and his parents worked the vaudeville circuit. Adorable

Young Dudley Riggs prepares for one of his early circus appearances with the Russell Brothers Circus in 1932, the year of his birth.

Dudley sang silly songs in city after city, and whenever he was introduced, it always seemed to be his debut and his birthday, too.

"I started performing in vaudeville as one of the Humanettes," he recalled. "They were small figures who performed in a small proscenium, mannequins with human heads doing a song and dance. That's where I mark my theatrical beginnings, being pushed onstage and told, 'Cover until they're ready.'"

But come spring, it was back to the circus. One such circus traveled to Japan after World War II, with the teenaged Dudley among the clowns.

"That tour was sponsored by the U.S. government to try to promote another view of America," he recalled. "So it was the first time that they'd ever had the circus."

Among the attendees was the emperor's son, Crown Prince Akihito. "I, not knowing the protocol, ended up being photographed shaking hands with him while I was dressed in my clown costume."

A flurry of press releases streamed forth from both the United States and Japanese governments about the controversy of this young American clown shaking hands with Akihito. Dudley was detained. Then, in a triumph of spin, the emperor declared that this was a great example of Japan reaching

In a gesture that stirred international controversy, Dudley Riggs shakes hands with Crown Prince Akihito after a performance in Japan shortly after World War II.

out to the West, the handshake with the clown being a rich symbol for the new Japan joining the modern world. Dudley was released.

After returning to the United States, he headed to New York City, where he started booking vaudeville and circus acts in theaters and cabarets in the early 1950s. It was there that he developed the idea of "instant theater." It was something like a mentalist working the crowd, but Riggs and his cohorts would ask audience members to blurt out names, places and things, and they'd create a scene on the spot from the suggestions. Ideally, the scene was a funny one. He called it "instant theater" because jazz musicians told him that they'd already claimed the word "improvisation," and he couldn't use it. So there.

Maybe it was because the road was in his blood or perhaps things were drying up in New York, but Dudley took his group of actors and vaudevillians on the road and hit several cities. The money finally ran out in Minneapolis. But that was OK, because Dudley had a girl in the Twin Cities whose acquaintance he wished to renew. Her name was Ruth. She was a Macalester College student who worked at Stefano's Pizza near Cedar and Riverside in Minneapolis.

The neighborhood was about as much of a countercultural hotbed as the city had at the time, and the "West Bank" of the Mississippi was starting to hop. So Dudley convinced Stefano's to let him start booking acts in its backroom. Theater, music, comedy, poetry readings—the performances grew so popular that Dudley, now married to Ruth, started looking for a place of his own to host them. He wanted a place where he could serve

Dudley Riggs with the espresso machine and antique cash register that followed him to each of his Café Espresso spaces, here pictured at 2605 South Hennepin Avenue in 1966.

pastries and coffee drinks. And Ruth would be overjoyed if he got the vintage espresso machine that he'd purchased in Italy out of their living room. She called it "that damn coffee pot."

The first Café Espresso was at 18 University Avenue Northeast. After opening in 1958, Dudley started booking various collections of comic and theatrical performers. That's why the sign still reads, "Brave New Workshop, Founded by Dudley Riggs in 1958." While that name didn't come up until three years later, he was nevertheless now an invariably bow tie–clad, espresso-slinging impresario. As Dudley has often said, he ran away from the circus to join a family. And he seemed to have found one.

Irv Letofsky working on a Brave New Workshop script by the front window at Café Espresso in the early 1960s. Letofsky was the company's chief writer, editor and sometimes director for its revues throughout the '60s.

5

MARCH BACKWARD INTO HISTORY; OR, AN INSIDE LOOK AT THE BACKSIDE OF THE '60s

By the 1960s, the Brave New Workshop was working off of scripts created by dozens of writers. What started as a way to get people to come in and buy coffee at 207 East Hennepin now was gaining a following, eventually expanding well beyond its originally planned Sunday-night slot to perform several shows a week.

Yet if Minneapolis was as dull as the company's creators claim, what did they find to write about? Well, Letofsky was the catalyst for much of it, and it often had a regional flair, as when they'd take on the vices of the vice squad, a group perpetually on the hunt for prostitutes that set itself up for a skewering when city government dubbed it "the morals squad." It inspired a memorable pantomime (with Sullivan providing piano) in which two men compete for the affections—or business?—of a woman at a bar before each character pulls out his or her badge. It also helped inspire the 1963 revues *Morals is a Six-letter Word* and *Of Mothers and Morals; or, My Mother was a Morals Squad.*

Letofsky's dry wit came through in his scripts, which were full of droll wordplay. He was clearly fascinated by human behavior and loved to write brief dialogues fueled by role reversal, a twist at the end of each causing you to reconsider a character's motivations. Discussing whether or not to have sex was a popular theme in these times when birth control pills had reframed the debate. An early twist-based sketch featured a leather-jacketed, street-tough social worker advising a clean-cut (but nevertheless murderous) honor student.

Yet Letofsky's best and funniest sketches came when he abandoned the understated in favor of fast-paced satire, like 1964's "The Bismarck People," in which hysteria spreads at a neighborhood cocktail party when someone reveals that her house has been sold to a couple from Bismarck, North Dakota. Other guests are soon gripped with fear, relaying to one another in panicked fashion all that they've heard about people from Bismarck: "They have big, vulgar cars and pink Princess phones." "They don't brush after meals." "They have sex orgies, crabgrass and build a lot of schools, which in turn raises property taxes."

A revue might be interspersed with commercials featuring two TV pitchmen from Kwickie Kulture Ink rapidly espousing their newest collection of the "50 greatest prayers" or "50 greatest sermons," taking aim at many a sacred cow along the way.

Dan Sullivan's style was a fine complement to Letofsky's, his scenes sometimes seeming warm-toned slices of life that would invite more smiles than guffaws. Like "Love in a Laundromat," which he said remains his favorite. He said:

> *It was about two University of Minnesota kids who had just met at the laundromat and the idea was that we went inside their minds and saw them gradually becoming interested in each other as a boy and a girl would, from doing their laundry together. He'd help her with her laundry, and they would sit there, watching the clothes dry and their heads would start to revolve while watching the clothing in the dryer and adding soap. But the boy was sort of clumsy and the girl was, too, so I think they put in too much soap and it went on the floor. And you had to imagine all this, for it was all done without props.*
>
> *There was also "Ben Lazy, Socialized Doctor," which was based on the idea that if you had universal medical care in a socialized state, then all of your health workers would be very lazy. I was always in favor of universal health care, but I didn't mind having a laugh about it. That's my very favorite bit of ours. These clumsy, crazy, lazy, not-at-all-interested-in-medicine people operating on a guy and they had to do a heart transplant. And they pulled out a big valentine's heart. You see, that's just how stupid we were.*

But it wasn't just stupid. Sullivan also had a strong interest in theater—he later became a drama critic for the *New York Times* and the *Los Angeles Times*—and Sir Tyrone Guthrie's new repertory company in

Minneapolis surely inspired some of his wonderful mash-ups of different classics. Like "Hamhock," which was *Hamlet* as if written by Tennessee Williams. And an *Oedipus*, in which the Greek tragedy was transported to upper-crust England and delivered by a tea-sipping Noel Coward couple.

> *Jocasta: Well, no, it's really nothing that serious. I'm sorry I brought it up.*
> *Oedipus: Ah, but, pet, I'm intrigued.*
> *Jocasta: No, no, no, it's nothing, really.*
> *Oedipus: Oh, well, if it's nothing…*
> *Jocasta: Well, the truth is—I'm your mother. Ha ha ha.*
> *Oedipus: Cigarette?*
> *Jocasta: Thank you. I meant to tell you sooner, of course.*
> *Oedipus: Oh, you mustn't blame yourself, darling. I suppose I ought to have noticed something.*

Among the cultural changes taking place that proved good skit fodder were:
- Sex education being introduced in the schools (with kids explaining to a parent group the askew information they had gleaned)
- Obscenity laws (a stuffy literary lecture on a bodice ripper novel)
- A government agent who alerts his superiors of an impending nuclear attack and finds that they are interested only in being set up on dates with his female co-workers.

And then there was "Dr. Oral Gross," a sketch built off the premise of a lecture about sex research, clearly inspired by the academic progeny of Dr. Alfred Kinsey and his ilk. It was a hilarious parody of analytical gobbledygook that ends up employing a lot of Groucho Marx–esque oratorical misdirection plays. As Dr. Gross gestures to one chart or human figure after another, he explains the basis of gender differences thus:

> *Gross: You'll notice in Chart 1 that we have Man, which is composed of a series of isosolistic triangulations with a strong K factor. This type of person has a unitized system consisting of a high-voltage horizontal deflection circuit, with a master base of a vertical amplifier and a keyed automatic gain control for finest local reception.*
>
> *Concentrically, we have in Chart 2, Woman, which is constructed from a combination of centripetal coordinates with a strong Max factor. Here again you have your simple utilized structure with a full power transformer and rectifier. This increases contrast and eliminates the high current surge during the initial warm-up periods. It has rim control for finer tuning, a*

Irv Letofsky laughs while Phil Johnson reads during a read-through of a Brave New Workshop script in 1966.

sensitized oscillator that provides for unequaled performance, uniformity and ease of maintenance...

Now, if in the right triangle, an altitude is drawn from the hypotenuse, then each leg of the triangle is a mean proportional between the hypotenuse and the adjacent segments. For our hypotheses here, we go to Pythagoras, who postulated this theorem all over the floor of his office. Sometimes on the walls, the ceilings and all over the place.

But the show that really put the Brave New Workshop on the popular culture radar in the Twin Cities area wasn't a collection of sketches but a longer-form work that turned into the company's biggest hit of the 1960s, one that was revived yearly, inspired a locally legendary prank and became a record album. It all started with an annual American institution in Atlantic City, New Jersey.

The cast of a 1970 incarnation of the Miss America show, *Everything You Always Wanted to Know About Miss America, But Were Afraid to Ask*. *Front, left to right*: Fred Keller, Jackie Ralph and Richard Cottrell. *Rear, left to right*: Diana Brenke, Nancy Steen and Becky Bailey.

6

MISS AMERICA VERSUS MISS ST. PAUL; OR, PAGEANT OF PULCHRITUDE

From this distance, the Miss America Pageant may look like low-hanging fruit, an easy target for satire. From our perch atop a we'd-like-to-think more enlightened twenty-first century, going after a contest that lumps together roughly half of the country's population and, by process of elimination, determines which of them is the fundamentally best human being might seem abhorrent. Of course, the herd is culled by age range and marital status, and physical attractiveness is a highly weighted percentage of the equation, evening gowns and swimsuits assisting in determining who has the consummate pulchritude.

You could call it a sketch that mushroomed. It started out as half of one revue in the Brave New Workshop's first year, but more and more of those "new ideas" kept coming up, and it expanded into the company's first full-length show. Up to then, the Workshop's work had been satirical, but now it was producing its first large-scale parody, a send-up in which each element of the subject was imitated and ridiculed. It started with a pair of rapidly bantering commentators on the small side stage as the piano music swelled and subsided.

> *John: Good evening, Mr. and Mrs. America…*
> *Mary: …and all the ships at sea…*
> *John: This is warm and fun-loving John Cameron-Crazy, along with…*
> *Mary: Mary Lou Maudlin of Willacoochee, Georgia, your beautiful and talented Miss America…*
> *John: And we'll be your delightful, delicious, delovely hosts…*
> *Mary: On this night of nights…*
> *John: With your show of shows…*

Mary: The Miss America Pageant!
John: Oh, Mary, Mary, Mary!
Mary: Oh, John, John, John! It's so excitin', it chokes me up and makes we want to gag, John.
John: To think of all these unsullied girls being sullied on this very stage tonight, Mary.
Mary: And the Great Hall here at the Café Espresso looks so elegant, John.
John: Wow, they've swept up the floor and dusted the musty furniture, Mary.
Mary: Elegant, John.
John: And look at those people, Mary. Look at that one.
Mary: Makes you wonder about people, John.
John: There are a lot of big, important people here, Mary, and a lot of little, tiny, common people right off the streets, Mary.
Mary: And there's lots and lots and lots of celebrities, John. Why there's the Miss America of 1922, John, still lovely, still adorable Miss Lilac Bushmeyer of Augratin, Idaho, John.
John: How does she do it, Mary? She's still as young and beautiful as an Idaho potato, Mary!
Mary: And there goes the 1960 Miss Congeniality, John, Miss Ginger Peachymeister. She was a popular one, John.
John: Everybody remembers her for her bright and positive attitude, Mary.
Mary: She just couldn't say no, John.

Soon, the festivities would be handed over to host Bert Barks, a master of mellifluent malapropisms fashioned after Miss America host Bert Parks.

"Yes, the Miss America Pageant is the Olympia, the Blue Ribbon Premium Budweiser of sweetness and light, charm and poise and beauty and brains—and tonight, ladies and gentlemen, we will present a phantasmagoria of beauty and brains that you will not believe and reject and refuse to accept!"

The evening proceeded to modeling evening gowns and swimsuits—Dayton's department store donated the swimsuits but insisted that its name not be mentioned—but the talent segment was what kept the premise from growing stale. Wild new performances were regularly inserted into the revue, from spoofs of operatic arias to a "Humoresque" on a zither (actually an autoharp, played by Anita Anderson) to outrageous, earnestly delivered poetry. (Miss California: "Sen. Goldwater, How much do I love thee?/Thy forthright manner of ignoring the facts…/March backward into history, for the future is filled with peril.") Customarily, there were three or four contestants, one of them always representing Minnesota to get the hometown crowd into the spirit.

Of course, that candidate would always win, leading to a Dan Sullivan–penned ceremonial song as she took her walk down the center aisle while

Barks intoned: "Yes, the quintessence of quality, the colossus of cleanliness, the dinosaur of decency, maidenhead of maidenhood…Yes, this is the one, the lone one, the sole, singular, solitary only one! Yes, all of the best of America—Teflon, Melmac, Tupperware, Brillo Pads and Diet Pepsi—all rolled into one grand and glorious girl!"

But then last year's Miss America would have a hard time surrendering her crown, and an onstage melee would ensue in which gowns and suits were shredded amid screams, punches, gouges and grabs borrowed from professional wrestling…while the theme music played on.

Some incarnation of the show made its way into the Brave New Workshop schedule for most of the 1960s, but it caused something of a sensation in 1962, thanks to media attention that wasn't the result of a review of the revue. Rather, it was an idea that the show inspired. Here is how writer/director Vince Williams remembered it:

> *After one of the performances, two guys asked to meet with us to discuss a "venture" they had in mind. They were from the St. Paul Jaycees, sponsor of the Miss St. Paul contest, which would, perhaps, "select" their candidate to move on to the Miss Minnesota cadre of contestants. The men informed us that rules for the Miss St. Paul contest were so lax that young women who entered the contest might be anyone from anywhere. There were no background checks or verifications of any kind that could corroborate information written on an application to enter the contest. In addition, a contestant's "talent" was not viewed ahead to help with a decision about legitimacy.*
>
> *One other very important rule of their contest was the talent portion provided one-half of all the contest points. The girl who won the talent couldn't lose the contest. So, it was their plan that we should have one of our actresses enter the contest and present her "talent." We viewed this as a prospect for great adventure.*
>
> *We chose Ruth Williams…As the director at Brave New Workshop at the time, I took her through several rehearsals of her song and informational intro to it. Additionally, Ruth didn't live in St. Paul, was married (to me) and was mother to a little girl. Ruth begged off of going to either of the two Miss St. Paul Contest rehearsals, explaining that her father had had a sudden attack, and she had to be with him in the hospital, an excuse that seemed acceptable to the contest director and all the Jaycees involved.*

Dudley recalled that they used Letofsky's St. Paul address on her application. Each time the contest officials called about something, Letofsky said that she was in the shower.

"So now we come to the evening of the contest," Vince Williams recalled.

> *There were thirty-two contestants other than Ruth, and she "presented" wearing a ballerina-like, knee-length dress while all the other girls had on floor-length formals. All thirty-two other girls presented their talent, and there were some that must be described as pitiful. One girl tap-danced to the music of "Danny Boy," as just an example.*
>
> *Ruth's piano accompanist was Ruth Riggs, Dudley's wife, and Ruth was one of the last to perform. She came out below the curtain line so they wouldn't be able to close the curtain on her.*

Irv Letofsky wrote her introduction for her. In his 2007 memoir, *Promiscuous Comedy*, he recounted how young "Alice Martin" (as she was dubbed) delivered it from the stage of the St. Paul Central High School auditorium:

> *This is a mournful little love song dedicated to my former boyfriend, now dead, named Herman, who was from Duluth and was killed in a terrible car accident not long ago. So this is dedicated to Herman, to his family and friends and to all people everywhere who might get killed in a bad car accident in the future or injured and their family and friends and many, many other people whether or not their names are Herman. (To pianist.) Hit it.*

"Alice" kept time by flapping her right arm and snapping her fingers as she sang this song by Dan Sullivan, which opened with several "ooh, ooh, oohs."

> *We're going steady, me and Herman Tate,*
> *Each night he comes to help me con-ju-gate*
> *My—German, ooh ooh ooh ooh, Herman!*
> *I don't mean Sherman, oh no.*
>
> *When I see Herman coming down the street*
> *He makes the other fellas that I meet*
> *Look like vermin, ooh ooh ooh ooh Herman!*
> *You make me feel like I was wearin' ermine, oh yes.*

The song went on for several verses. Company member Perry Cucchiarella was assigned to sit in the audience and report back whatever happened. He said that, with the first "ooh, ooh, oohs," the snickers grew to guffaws from about half of the five hundred people present, while the other half glared at them.

Covering the pageant were *Minneapolis Tribune* reporters Ken Jumper and Dick Cunningham, who seized on the unusual atmosphere during Williams's performance. According to their story, the pageant judges were "frozen-faced at first" before "one couldn't contain his mirth any longer and exploded in laughter." One judge was quoted thus: "She was kidding, wasn't she? I mean you can't tell. Some people are awful cuckoo." Another said, "If it was serious, I'm glad I didn't laugh. But if she was being funny, I wish that I had."

The whole scam was uncovered by the next day, with the two schemers disciplined by the Jaycees. Ruth Williams found the whole experience pretty stressful. As she recounted in Letofsky's memoir:

> *I guess I felt I was betraying some of the legitimate contestants: poor, innocent young women who looked upon me as a pathetic creature. Although they were my competition, they were very nice, offering to do things like paint my fingernails and give advice about my hair and what jewelry I should wear. They felt sorry for me and I felt so guilty, thinking: "If you only knew."*
>
> *But, during my performance, while I was singing ridiculous lyrics and shocking rhymes with vocal stresses to go along with my dramatic finger snapping, I was truly surprised that not many people seemed to be angry with me. It appeared as though half of the audience was howling with laughter and the other half felt really pathos.*
>
> *I also remember the program's stage manager running in my direction, saying "Let me at her!" But I didn't stay around long for the aftermath.*

Indeed, Vince Williams was waiting in a car near the stage door with the engine running. But Ruth did win a special talent award. The *Tribune* story—"City Housewife in Miss St. Paul Contest as Hoax"—exposed the prank.

"It left us all kind of stunned," Dudley recalled. "But it generated a tremendous amount of...There were fights and people kicked off committees. It sort of kept itself stirring. So more people heard about the *Miss America* show, and it became much more of a money maker for us."

It also became a record album. It's hard to find now, but it was a relative hit when one thousand copies were released (at a sold-out Brave New Workshop) on July 3, 1963. By the time some members of the cast headed to Atlantic City that September to hawk copies of the album, it was up to thirty thousand copies in distribution.

Oh, by the way, the young woman who defeated Ruth Williams at the Miss St. Paul Pageant in late '62, Sharon Carnes, was Miss Minnesota at the '63 Miss America Pageant.

Congressman Clark MacGregor works the ample crowd assembled at the old Café Espresso, 207 East Hennepin Avenue, for one of his 1963 performances with Brave New Workshop. *Courtesy of the* Star Tribune.

7

THE POLITICAL INVITATIONAL; OR,
FARR, FORSYTHE AND
OTHER FARCES

P romiscuous hostility, positive neutrality"—that was what Dudley and company adopted as the Brave New Workshop's motto early on. Dudley was intent on the comedy being as hostile to one political viewpoint as another but also wanted to be positive enough to leave audiences smiling. As its buzz grew, politicians started expressing interest in participating in Brave New Workshop shows. One of the first was the congressman from Minnesota's third congressional district, Republican Clark MacGregor, who saw it as a good place for a 1962 campaign stop while running for reelection.

Granted, he didn't represent Minneapolis but its western and northern suburbs, so who knows how many actual or potential constituents he'd have in the house? But MacGregor had been itching to get back on stage ever since his theatrical days at Dartmouth College, so Letofsky and a handful of other writers provided him with a script that proved a solid send-up of a life in politics.

In one sketch, he prepared in fidgeting fashion to meet with someone from *Time* magazine, arranging the American flags on his desk for maximum visual effect and muttering nervously about the possibility of making the cover. After admonishing himself with "Be calm, cover boy," he greeted the *Time* rep, who, after sitting down, said, "Now, about your subscription…"

He also played a mayoral candidate who delivered a speech in which he animatedly said, "I love this town. I'll get this town moving again. And I'll make the same promise as long as there is a breath in my body!" and "We've all heard a lot of filthy lies about the mayor…but I'm afraid that we just don't have the time here tonight to repeat all of them and give them all the consideration that they deserve."

At evening's end, Dudley said that the appearance was no endorsement, "But we thank Alderman Bob MacGregor for being here

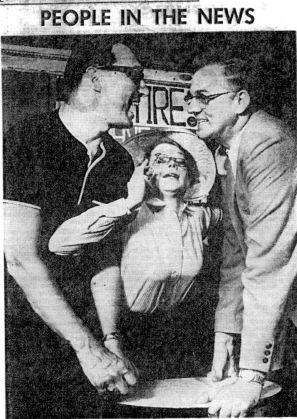

2   MINNEAPOLIS TRIBUNE ★ Tues., June 1, 1965

PEOPLE IN THE NEWS

Minneapolis Tribune Photo by Powell Krueger

GEORGE FARR, left, Minnesota DFL chairman, squared off against ROBERT FORSYTHE, state GOP chairman, Monday night in a political "free-for-all" during a satirical sketch at Dudley Riggs' Cafe Espresso, 207 E. Hennepin Av. MRS. RUTH WILLIAMS, 445 4th Av. NE., tried to break them up as they "debated" the actions of the Minnesota Legislature "and other political abuses." Title of the sketch was "Farr, Forsythe and Other Farces."

STAR June 1 '65

BARBS FLY

Politician in Satire Session

Should Minnesota Governor Karl Rolvaag sell his Lincoln to balance the budget?

Is it fun for legislators to raise state income taxes and at the same time double their salaries?

These were two of the barbed questions posed Monday night when real-life politicians joined the Brave New Workshop satirical troupe before a packed house at Dudley Riggs' Cafe Expresso.

Robert Forsythe, state GOP chairman, and George Farr, state DFL chairman, portrayed each other in a "great debate."

Farr offered his version of Forsythe's defense of the sales tax: The poorer families can get by without paying a cent of sales tax "if they don't buy a house, a car or any appliances, clothes or food."

Forsythe, playing the role of Farr, retaliated with a prediction that Gov. Rolvaag will continue to get elected "again and again and again and again — until he does the job right."

Other targets during the review included:

St. Paul Mayor George Vavoulis—considered a likely candidate for governor because he "usually runs at least an hour ahead of everyone else."

Secretary of Agriculture Orville Freeman — "You show me a man who doesn't think Orv Freeman is a great secretary of agricultre, and I'll show you a farmer."

The chair of Minnesota's Democratic (DFL) Party, George Farr (left), is separated from state Republican chair Robert Forsythe (right) by Ruth Williams in a photo accompanying a June 1, 1965 *Minneapolis Tribune* article about the Brave New Workshop revue *Farr, Forsythe and Other Farces. Courtesy of the* Star Tribune.

tonight." However, MacGregor had started a trend that would lead to other politicians appearing on the Brave New Workshop stage, including another congressman (and later mayor), Don Fraser, Minneapolis mayor Art Naftalin and the 1964 Republican candidate for U.S. senator, Wheelock Whitney. After St. Paul mayor George Vavoulis appeared in a show, Dudley said to the crowd, "St. Paul doesn't really exist. It was made up by F. Scott Fitzgerald."

Dudley recalled, "We came up with the idea of having a periodic fundraiser for the League of Women Voters that I called the Brave New Workshop Political Invitational. The concept was that we would invite opposing candidates to come in and play each other. And we would script it for those debates."

That led to *Farr, Forsythe and Other Farces*, a "debate" in which Robert Forsythe, head of the state's Republican Party, traded roles and barbs with George Farr, chair of the state's Democratic-Farmer-Labor Party. (In Minnesota, the Democrats merged with the Farmer-Labor Party, which was successful enough to have had three governors elected in the 1930s.)

"I loved being able to put them in opposition," Dudley said, "and they loved it. We had Hubert [Humphrey, a U.S. senator at the time] interested but were never able to quite get him. And they enjoyed the challenge. So the spirit was there, and I thought it a worthwhile tradition. 'Look at Minneapolis, where the politicians can have fun with each other.'"

The fact that he didn't make it to Brave New Workshop didn't keep Humphrey from appearing in the troupe's revues. Well, not him, exactly, but a reasonable facsimile named Sen. Humfff, a loquacious purveyor of stem-winder speeches with a style a lot like that of Minnesota's notoriously talkative senior senator and then U.S. vice president and then junior senator. In a typical Letofsky-penned speech, Sen. Humfff concluded his stirring remarks by saying, as patriotic music surged beneath him:

> *And so, fellow Americans, it's time we rolled up our sleeves and pulled down our pants…And as we march off into the horizon, shoulder to shoulder, arm to arm, nose to nose, the burden heavy on our back, we must pull ourselves up by the bootstrap, put our shoulder on the wheel, our nose on the grindstone, our teeth on the nail, our eye on the bouncing ball…*

Or a show would feature a perennial gadfly candidate who would say of his opponent: "I can beat him any day of the week, except maybe Tuesdays."

In the alley behind Cafe Espresso, Congressman MacGregor studied his satire script while other Brave New Workshop actors rehearsed a script. MacGregor worried over his lines, pacing the alley. In one sketch he played a mayor running for re-election. Asked if he "enjoyed" police brutality, the "mayor" replied, "Many times I've told the police chief, 'Chief, ya gotta be careful who ya knock around.'" His opponent said, "We've all heard a lot of filthy lies about the mayor . . . but I'm afraid we just don't have the time here tonight to repeat all of them."

Congressman Clark MacGregor goes over his script in the alley behind 207 East Hennepin in 1963 while Dudley Riggs rehearses other actors behind him. *Courtesy of the Star Tribune.*

Politics has always been a prime focus for the Brave New Workshop, as evidenced by such '60s titles as *The Lyndon Frolics: Great Fables from the Great Society* and its recurring spoof of the American electoral process, *Yankee Doodle Dum Dum: The Resistible Rise of the Last Honest Man*. Soon thereafter came a 1972 revue that asked the hypothetical question of whether President Nixon might have known about the Watergate break-in, *The Future Lies Just Ahead*, and the post–Nixon-landslide show, *In Search of a Cause; or, What's Left for the Left?*

"We remained suspect for quite a while," Dudley said. "But I think maybe the political shows gave us some good association, in that, well, if Mayor [Art] Naftalin's in it, it must be OK."

When it was pointed out to him by a *Minneapolis Tribune* reporter that members of both parties accused him of supporting the other side, Dudley said, "Which proves, I suppose, that paranoia knows no parties."

Tom Sherohman and Anita Anderson as characters representing militaristic and pro-peace views in a promotional image for 1968's *The Not-Quite All-Over Show*.

8

SILLY, SPONTANEOUS AND SOUTHBOUND; OR, SABU, SADDLE UP THE ELEPHANTS

Stupid stuff.

That's what Pat Proft said he brought to the Brave New Workshop. Amid the clever social satire, commentary on race relations and punishing of politicians, Proft joined the company and bravely made a stand for dumb humor.

It started at his audition, where the freshly minted Columbia Heights High School grad was asked to improvise a scene in a hospital and started by miming holding something away from his body while hurrying down a hallway. Upon colliding with another actor, his hand opened, his eyes hit the floor and he yelled, "Oh, no, the specimen!"

That was Pat Proft. He was always more into parody than satire; that is, he loved to spoof stuff, throwing in some physical shtick as if he walked off a turn-of-the-century vaudeville stage and into a time machine that landed him in mid-'60s Minneapolis.

"It was so great," Proft recalled. "For me, someone who wanted to do comedy since as long as I can remember. I grew up on Laurel and Hardy and the Marx Brothers and the Three Stooges and Little Rascals. It's all I wanted to do, so it was wonderful. And I think that we were one of the first groups that started doing our own material, of bringing things into the shows. We started improvising stuff."

His chief partner in crime was Tom Sherohman. Together, they developed characters that became staples of sketches. People like Captain Cookies.

"I was Captain Cookies, a children's show host," Proft said. "And Tom was a neighbor. It went on for like five, six, seven minutes, and Phil Johnson came in at the end as the guy with the seal or something like that."

"He had a walrus," Sherohman interjected.

Proft continued:

> Then we started to do more of that in rehearsals, where we would start to bring an idea in. I always wanted to do a pickpocket on his first job, so Tom was my victim, and he had some pants that I would just totally rip to shit. It was a great, stupid little visual bit. And I think that's something that Tom, me and [Michael] McManus brought to the place was this visual, physical humor. We certainly loosened it up a little bit more. We weren't as into intellectual stuff as Irv wanted.
>
> Like I'd put a toilet seat over Tom's head, kiss him and say, "Welcome to Poland." That got a big laugh in 1968. Just stupid things like that. Then we did the Supremo Brothers, which I think was one of my favorite things to do. It was always a second-half bit. It would get longer each night as we screwed around with it. The idea was that I was... Sargasso Supremo?

"I was Sargasso. You were Rudolfo." Sherohman said.

"We were circus performers, and we were doing stupid tricks like something where you'd light a match and I'd blow it out? And that would be the fire trick. But the big thing is that I would do the kiss of passion. Which we'd try to get someone from the audience..."

"Rudolfo Supremo, the world's greatest lover."

"That was it." Proft said.

> I was the world's greatest lover. And I would try to get someone from the audience, but I would eventually end up doing it with Ruth [Williams]. I'd give her a big kiss, and while I was kissing her, I'd be blowing up a beach ball in her stomach. And the lights would be going crazy and I'd be puff, puff, puff doing that, and I'd turn around and "Oh, my god!" She'd be pregnant instantly. Then we'd have a wedding ceremony. What did you say? "Sabu, saddle up the elephants. We ride tonight?" But then Dudley would come out and marry us. He'd give us a ring. It was amazingly silly, and it got just great laughs. A big, stupid and, of course, very satirical piece.
>
> Tom would have ideas; I would have ideas; McManus, when he was in the group, he'd have ideas. So we'd all just bring them in, and I remember sitting down when we'd start a new show, and you'd get a packet of what

Pat Proft and Tom Sherohman in 1968's look at American involvement in Vietnam, *The Not-Quite All-Over Show.*

the scripts were going to be like and what the theme was going to be like. And you'd read through them, and everyone had his ideas that fit the theme. A pickpocket…what theme is that going to fit? So Irv had to find a way to make that fit into the show. "Times are so bad that…people are turning to crime." There you go, so now it's satirical.

Michael McManus said, "In one show, Pat and I did a bit where I burned my draft card and set it in an ash tray."

Proft recalled, "I set the table wrong and it was three legs on the stage and one off. So, when we did the bit, the thing fell over and the guy in the front row had his pants on fire for a minute."

Proft's tenure started in 1965 in the narrow little room at 207 East Hennepin. But soon, he and the rest of Brave New Workshop went south.

"The thing about the move to 2605 is that me and McManus were in the show," Proft said.

Brave New Workshop's longtime home at 2605 South Hennepin Avenue, pictured in 2002.

And then the week before, Dudley said, "Hey, I think we'll be moving." We thought that was funny, and we laughed. And McManus and I thought he was kidding, and he wasn't. No one called us about the actual move. So Mike and I pull up to the theater and it said, "We have moved." And it's like eight minutes before show time. So we go to 2605 and Dudley and Ruth are putting up newspapers in the window to keep the light out so we can do blackouts. And we got ready for a show and put chairs down, and I think that four or five people showed up.

How did this move to 2605 South Hennepin Avenue in November 1965 happen so quickly? Dudley Riggs explained:

On a Friday, I went before a judge who said be out of the building by midnight Sunday. So we did that weekend show, and, on Sunday night, everything was loaded in a truck, and we left that location. So then the tech man, Paul Stenbock, and I had a rental truck full of stuff and no place to put it. And it was cold weather, we couldn't do a garage sale. And the cost of the truck was going up every day. And so Stenbock and I were seated in Embers [a restaurant] at Twenty-sixth and Hennepin, and we saw a guy putting a sign up in the window across the street. So I went over and talked to him. He was in big trouble and needed a tenant badly. So we cut the deal on Wednesday and on Thursday we moved the stuff in. We always said we'll present the Brave New Workshop every Friday and Saturday night. We managed to get the word out to most of the actors, but some didn't get the word until the day of the show, Friday. And they came over, and we did the show. And it ran pretty damn well, considering. Fortunately, we had the touring company lights, so we were able to set those up and get the show up.

During the following week, I sat down and discussed the whole thing with the cast and determined that I could pay them a salary if they could continue and were interested. And I said I'd like them to do the next show. And so we contracted them to do the next show.

I think I put Brave New Workshop where it should have been from the beginning. The original Café Espresso on University, which was an eviction. And 207 East Hennepin, that was an eviction. So I was getting tired of being right in front of the wrecking ball. It was like, "Hey, that's a nice looking building, I bet it's cheap." They'd say, "Well, you can have it for a while, but it's either going to be coming down or will be redeveloped." So that was a kind of foolish way of doing business. You didn't want to start an institution under such circumstances, but I always thought that I'd only do that for a year or two and then go back on the road.

One of the first shows at 2605 was *The Second Greatest Story Ever Told*, in which Sherohman portrayed Jesus returned to Earth and visiting Minneapolis.

"That show may have had the greatest ending ever at the Brave New Workshop," Proft recalled. "Tom was to ascend to Heaven. And he stepped into the elevator—there was an elevator onstage at 2605—and, while looking upward, he went down, saying, 'Wait a minute! Hey!' It got a huge laugh."

Sherohman revived the character in 1967's *The Almighty Revue; or, You Can't Keep a Good Man Down*. That led to some angry church groups (and the inevitable brick through the window), but Sherohman, who at one time had studied for the Catholic priesthood, maintained in a 1967 *Minneapolis Star* article, "If anyone leaves thinking less of Jesus, then we have failed. Our target in this satire is not Jesus. What we're criticizing is the hypocrisy that has eaten into organized religion. People who argue blasphemy are saying that Christ, his teachings and the church are inseparable. We don't feel that way."

Tom Sherohman portraying Jesus in 1967's *The Almighty Revue; or, You Can't Keep a Good Man Down*, a look at what might happen if Jesus visited modern Minneapolis.

That sounds like a serious approach for a show in which Jesus takes the Minnesota Multiphasic Personality Inventory and is determined to have a messiah complex. But what Jesus found in *The Almighty Revue* was a lot of talk about being Christian but very little action in keeping with Jesus's teachings. Sketches at the Brave New Workshop were also starting to take a more jaundiced view of increased American involvement in Vietnam. In *The Almighty Revue*, Jesus visited General William Westmoreland, commander of U.S. military operations in Vietnam. When Jesus asked if he had no compassion for those who were suffering in the war, Westmoreland replied, "I looked out over those fields of destruction, and I thought about all of the innocent women and children who would be killed, hurt, mutilated, and I thought about how sad their little faces would be. Sir, that's compassion."

Local theater critics called it the best show in the company's history. But scenes like that—and such shows as 1966's *The 143rd Annual Foreign Intervention Revue; or, The Vietnam Follies* and 1967's *The Not-Quite All-Over Show*—also caused more bricks through the window, Green Berets dropping by to aggressively lambast the staff and other problems.

Pat Proft said, "*The Vietnam Follies*, that's where we all got in trouble. Some people got audited, and I was told that I had enlisted in the Marines. I got a piece of paper saying that, which wasn't right. I had to get lawyers and things, and they screwed with me for a long time. They came down kind of hard on the cast, I thought."

Topicality was also there in Riggs's nightly newspaper-aided monologues, but he started to move away from those.

"When I got there, in '65, it was very heavy Dudley and Irv," Proft said. "And then it became more Irv. And then Jim Wallace got involved. Irv, Jim and then Dudley was still doing the monologue. And he still had one of the best lines: 'World War One—a big mistake.'"

"Archduke Ferdinand found alive in Argentina," Sherohman replied.

And Riggs's idea of "instant theater" was starting to re-emerge as Proft, Sherohman and company started doing late-night all-improvisation shows.

Proft said, "Probably after ten o'clock on Fridays and Saturdays. We did eight o'clock on Tuesday, Wednesday, Thursday. Friday, we also had a ten o'clock show. On Saturday, eight, ten and fricking midnight. And we'd get like thirty-five, forty people, so why not? In the summer, the audience was great. The audience was a high school, college kind of audience, so we had a young crowd, which was great."

As Julius Novick of the New York–based *Village Voice* said on attending a performance of 1966's *The Second Annual Race Riot Revue: Black Like Them*:

> *The Brave New Workshop is important not because it's good, but because it's there. The material is not first-rate, but it comes out of the community and it relates to the community. As a visitor, I enjoyed it, more or less; but I think that if I were a kid going to high school or perhaps college in Minneapolis, the Workshop…might have meant a great deal to me. Relevance, irreverence and sex talk combined make a heady brew for an adolescent, and I think a healthy one.*

Indeed, Dudley estimated in a 1967 *Minneapolis Tribune* article that "about 70 percent of our viewers are university or high school students." The increasingly youthful following led to the start of something like a farm team. In the fall of 1967, Brave New Workshop held auditions for a youth troupe called the Undersubcommittee, and seventy students showed up. Response was so strong that they ended up forming a second group, the Doubleundersubcommittee. The members of each group participated in improvisation workshops and performed a weekly half-hour

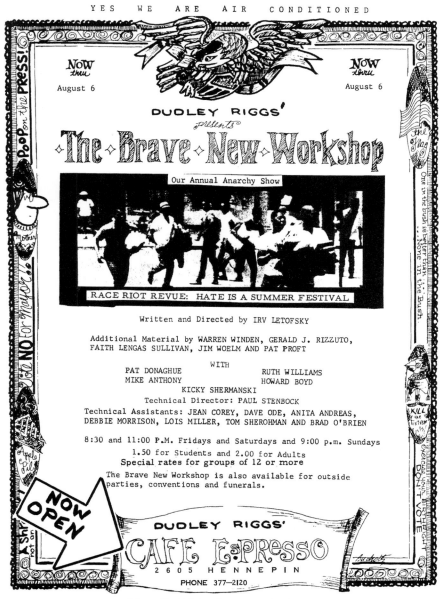

The program for the 1967 show *Race Riot Revue: Hate is a Summer Festival*, a biting satire of race relations in the Twin Cities area and beyond.

show—the Undersubcommittee on Wednesdays and Thursdays and the Doubleundersubcommittee on Sundays.

The Minneapolis Council of Churches asked Dudley in for a meeting. They presented statistics about how many thousands of people under the age of twenty-five lived in the neighborhood around Brave New Workshop. They wanted to know why they were going to his theater instead of church. And they wanted to borrow his mailing list.

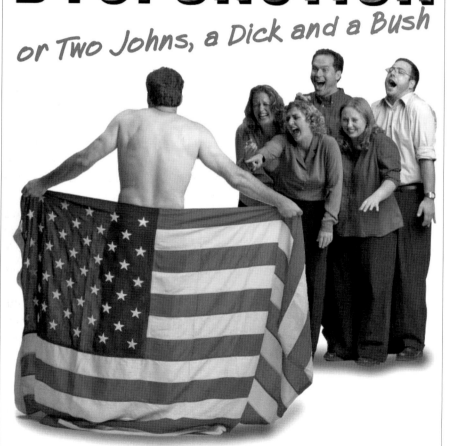

The Brave New Workshop Comedy Theatre
presents our 248th comedy revue:

ELECTILE DYSFUNCTION

or Two Johns, a Dick and a Bush

We're the Brave New Workshop, and we approve this message.

In 2004, the company found the names of the Republican and Democratic nominees for president and vice president to be good fodder for a title.

9

THE TITULAR ROUNDUP; OR, NOW THAT WE HAVE YOUR ATTENTION...

W e'll get back to our story in a minute, but this seems like a good time to talk a bit about something Minnesotans have come to expect from the Brave New Workshop over the years: a really catchy title. Wandering the streets in a headstand on top of his father's head, Dudley Riggs surely learned early that you get an audience by grabbing people's attention. While Brave New Workshop participated in its share of antics to alert potential ticket buyers to its work, many clever, eye-catching titles have put the company's name on people's lips, even if they don't end up seeing the show. The titles alone became local jokes.

The troupe has often started creating a new show by coming up with a title and building from there. Sometimes the theme has come first, sometimes not. But here's some of the wittiest wordplay employed in Brave New Workshop titles over the course of its half-century-plus of performances.

Hot Flashes on the Arctic Tundra (1971)
Dudley has always had a commitment to comedy that addresses a woman's point of view.

Overdrawn at the Sperm Bank (1972)
Artificial insemination, "test tube babies" and the whole brave new world of science-assisted parenting was examined.

Mary Tyler Moore Never Slept Here (1974)

Yes, *The Mary Tyler Moore Show* may have been set in Minneapolis, but…

Today is the Last Day of Your Life, So Far (1976)

Every aphorism is eligible for twisting, in this case the bright becoming bleak…or not, depending on how your life's gone, so far.

Love the One You Whip (1976)

Ah, the '70s, when sadomasochism was first noticed by mainstream pop culture.

Dow Jones Goes Down for Anybody (1979)

That was certainly true in 1979, when America was going through a severe economic downturn that contributed to Jimmy Carter losing his reelection bid the next year.

How Much Does This Holocaust?; or, Armageddon Out of Here (1979)

That's right, kids, many of us grew up accustomed to the idea that we could all be vaporized at any moment.

Future Tense; or, Rubbered Bothered Baby Boomers (Survival Tips for the Rest of the Future) (1988)

Sex has been a staple subject at the Workshop since its earliest days, but things got complicated with the AIDS pandemic and outbreaks of STDs. People were getting…tense.

The Girth of a Nation; or, Alice Doesn't Work Out Here Anymore (1988)

Fitness is in. No, wait, it's out. This is the revue that posited that being a couch potato could be sexy.

Mad in the USA; or Riot, You'll Like It (1992)

The Workshop tapped into the surly tenor of the populace in post–Gulf War America.

Your Accountability is Overdrawn (1992)

Ethics was the focus of a revue in which a lounge crooner sang of the need to prove yourself disease-free before becoming physical.

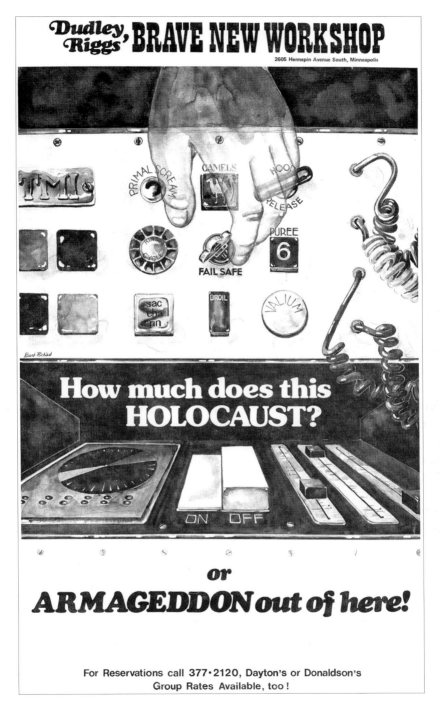

A poster for the 1979 production *How Much Does This Holocaust?; or, Armageddon Out of Here!*

When same-sex marriage became legal in Minnesota in 2013, the topic was explored in that year's holiday show, with Tom Reed and Matt Erkel appearing on the poster.

Politically Correct Means Always Having to Say You're Sorry (1993)
Before it became a tiresome cliché most often used as a right-wing pejorative, "politically correct" was often about making sure that you were burdening yourself with the proper amount of liberal guilt.

Saving Clinton's Privates; or, Swallow the Leader (1998)
Whether the presidential peccadilloes were worth an impeachment is a matter of debate, but they certainly led to some pretty prurient congressional testimony.

Electile Dysfunction; or, Two Johns, a Dick and a Bush (2004)
Speaking of prurient: who would think that Messrs. Kerry and Edwards matching up against Bush and Cheney could inspire something like this?

Manger Crashers; or, Three Wise Guys with a Pack of Camels (2005)
Another way to look at the Magi making the Bethlehem scene and one of the best holiday revue titles.

Pluto and Other Lies My Teacher Told Me (2007)
When scientists decided that our solar system had eight planets, not nine, the troupe started asking what else we've taken for granted that will turn out not to be true.

The Lion, the Witch and the War Hero; or, Is McCain Able? (2008)
By the time this presidential election year revue was on the boards, the field had narrowed to Barack Obama, Hilary Clinton and John McCain.

Spilling Me Softly; or, When the Gulf Goes Black, It Never Goes Back (2010)
And then there was the Deepwater Horizon oil spill that gushed on for months, which provided some humor as dark as the water.

Toyota! The Runaway Musical Hit! (2010)
Underlining the Riggs motto that nothing is sacred save the circus, accidents caused by unintended acceleration inspired this title.

I Saw Daddy Marry Santa Claus (2013)
Marriage equality being signed into law in Minnesota brought a new perspective to the 2013 holiday revue.

Ann Ryerson and Michael McManus in *Lovers and Other Mothers*, a revue performed at the new ETC space in 1972.

10

THE ACCIDENTAL EMPIRE; OR, EAST TO THE WEST BANK

Remember that "instant theater" idea that Dudley Riggs had way back when? It turned out to have some legs after all. But moving toward building shows out of improvisation was partially an economic decision.

Dudley said, "When we moved to South Hennepin, we started paying them something. So now I had salaried actors, and I couldn't really afford salaried writers, so we started moving into the writer/actor creation process."

Brave New Workshop had become very popular, although its crowds were spread out over nine shows a week. Yet the theater always seemed intimate, thanks to hanging partitions that could be moved in to shrink the room. The walls closed in, if you will. But moving walls almost contributed to the moving of the Brave New Workshop. Dudley recalled:

> *The idea was that the iron cross and hot rod store was taking the rent, but they didn't really approve of what we were doing. But they had their business, which involved taking truckload shipments of racing tires and storing them in the theater until they had use for them. So we found ourselves coming up on show time, and the theater was full of tires. So I complained about that, and the next time I came in, the green room had been reduced from about twenty-four feet to about fourteen. They just moved our little wall. And our lease was coming up for renewal. So I thought, well, maybe this is time for us to look for a new space. So I ended up going to Seven Corners* [in Minneapolis's West Bank neighborhood near the University of Minnesota] *and signed a lease there.*

The new space was in the old Brite Spot Bar at 1430 South Washington Avenue, just a few blocks away from where Dudley first presented shows at Stefano's Pizza.

However, instead of closing one shop and opening another, Dudley ended up with two theaters. "When the hot rod store said, 'I've just renewed your lease,' I said, 'Well, what the hell am I going to do now?' So I figured that I would, for a while, run shows at both and then taper it off and move all the shows to the other theater."

That didn't happen. The new space became the venue for Brave New Workshop revues when it opened in 1971 under the name Brave New Workshop Also (soon changed to Dudley Riggs' ETC, for "Experimental Theater Company"). While the company was finding new audiences in the larger space at Seven Corners, the old following was firmly ensconced at 2605 South Hennepin and wasn't budging.

Doubling the Brave New Workshop output proved a challenge, as cast member Ann Ryerson—freshly graduated from Chicago's Northwestern University in the summer of 1971—remembered. She auditioned and got into a workshop. Then,

> *Three weeks into the workshop, which I think was almost daily,* [director] *Paul Menzel announced that Dudley was opening a new theater at Seven Corners and that five of us were to open a show in the old theater at Twenty-sixth and Hennepin so the current cast could open the new theater. Three weeks later, the five of us opened a revue show,* The Day the Muzak Stopped. *I want to emphasize that it had been only six weeks from being cast in the workshop to opening a show with four other neophytes: Sherri Luboff, Len Medrud, Jeff Woodward and Tom Davis.*
>
> *I had an idea for* The Day the Muzak Stopped *about two guys sitting on a bench and one asks the other for matches to light his cigarette, they start talking about a girl both had met at the restaurant named on the matches, and they find they've been dating the same girl. Tom Davis and Jeff Woodward took the kernel of the idea but went off in a completely different direction with it. The matches became the connection for them to realize they'd once been the same person, but at a fork in the road of life, one had become a businessman, the other an artist. The scene became more of a "head trip," but it was so extraordinarily acted by Tom and Jeff.*

It wasn't long before Dudley had second thoughts about running two theaters.

"After three years," he said, "I thought, 'My god, I have effectively divided the market.' I thought that the Seven Corners space would basically subsidize the other one, and it turned out to be the reverse."

"We opened our next show, *Lovers and Other Mothers*, at the new theater on Seven Corners," Ryerson recalled.

> *It had an old tin ceiling in the restaurant lobby and a beautiful big room to perform in. I loved the size (big) of the Washington Avenue theater compared to the Hennepin Avenue theater. You could really move on it. Tom Davis cooked omelets in the lobby restaurant during the dinner hour. Dudley was now even more distracted—he had two theaters and a restaurant to run!*

"For a couple of years, we kind of took on all comers," Dudley said. "We did Bertolt Brecht, lots of things that weren't satirical, and then that eventually involved stand-up comics. But I didn't start out to own a stand-up club and didn't particularly enjoy that process...It was all about finding an audience. And audiences hooked on stand-up comedy eventually."

In the early '70s, Tom Davis would spend summers reuniting with Al Franken—his old high school friend from the Minneapolis suburb of St. Louis Park—to perform two-man shows at 2605 Hennepin when Franken was home from Harvard. In addition to presenting their act in Los Angeles and New York, they also pitched themselves to a new late-night NBC venture called *Saturday Night Live* and were hired as part of its first writing staff in 1975. The following summer, they returned to ETC as Emmy-winning comedy writers and included in their act some of the sketches they'd written for *SNL*.

Taking "all comers" also meant revues built around the writings of Ogden Nash and Robert Benchley, comedies by Jules Feiffer and Woody Allen and a reenactment of some circa-1950 House Un-American Activities Committee hearings. It meant booking offbeat comedy acts from elsewhere for multi-week runs, like Paul Menzel (a former Brave New Workshop artistic director) and his Houston-based troupe, the Comedy Workshop; an early incarnation of comic magicians Penn and Teller (with a third accomplice; they called themselves "the Asparagus Valley Cultural Society"); comical jugglers the Flying Karamazov Brothers; and Duck's Breath Mystery Theater, now known for its public radio "Dr. Science" shorts.

Dudley had long wanted to own a restaurant, and Café Espresso, the restaurant within ETC, was getting very positive reviews from *Mpls./St. Paul Magazine* and the alternative weekly, the *Twin Cities Reader*.

Comedian Louie Anderson around the time he was launching his standup comedy career at Dudley Riggs' ETC in the 1970s.

But it was stand-up comedy that made ETC a destination. It started to take off when Louie Anderson started performing there in the late '70s, and he recorded his first comedy album there in 1980. He soon convinced Dudley to bring others on board.

Jeff Cesario recalled:

> *I was a budding stand-up in Minneapolis when Dudley decided to give the Seven Corners location to Louie Anderson for a month while the touring company was on the road. Louie formed the Minneapolis Comedy All Stars—Louie, Alex Cole, Joel Madison and myself. We were just so damn young, but Louie already had a showman's instinct. He worked the press like a political frontman, and when he and I pulled up in his old powder blue Mercury for opening night, there was a line around the block. It is still one of the great thrills of my show business career, including my first* Tonight Show *with Johnny* [Carson] *and my first Emmy for* Dennis Miller Live.

Dudley said:

> *The guys who were just starting in stand-up just had about three places in town where they could do it, but then we had a period where everybody in town had a stand-up club. And a lot of people who could do it one night a week all of a sudden wanted to do it as a full-time job. It's never been something where you could develop the loyalties of a group of people in one location...If you're in stand-up, you have to go and get another booking, so there's no way to build on that. We built on it a little bit with* What's So Funny About Being Female? *We were the only one offering that opportunity. A stand-up club owner in St. Paul said that the reason we don't have women on stage is because they weren't funny. But I answered that.*

What's So Funny About Being Female? was an evening of stand-up comedy by a collection of Twin Cities–based women. It proved very popular, debuting as *The Comedy Vixens* in 1983 and then running annually from 1986 until 1991. Among the performers were comedians Susan Vass and Lizz Winstead, the latter going on to become co-creator and head writer for TV's *The Daily Show*.

"It had such wonderful predictability," Dudley said. "You could open it the first of the year and then close it on Mother's Day or around the fishing opener."

Dudley Riggs' ETC is subjected to divine wrath in the poster for its 1980 revue *Side by Side by Sodom*.

Dudley felt strongly about women's rights:

> *It had always been my dad's policy that my mother would get equal billing as Riggs and Riggs and equal pay! In other show business families of those days, the wife usually worked for free. The family policy of Riggs and Riggs was that both my mother and father received equal pay and equal billing. So it was natural that I paid women the same as the guys at the Brave New Workshop from the beginning—and that, in the 1980s, I produced shows that showed that women could be just as funny as men.*

By early 1988, Minneapolis was something of an epicenter for the stand-up comedy boom. As Colin Covert wrote in the *Star Tribune*:

> *The area supports eight full-time comedy clubs: David Wood's Rib Tickler, Dudley Riggs' ETC Theatre, Uptown's new Funny Bone, the Ha Ha Club,* [Scott] *Hansen's Minneapolis, Maplewood and Bloomington clubs* [the Comedy Gallery] *and That Comedy Place, which opened above JR's Restaurant in Minneapolis when Hansen moved his club to Riverplace* [in the Near Northeast neighborhood where Brave New Workshop began]. *The clubs have a combined seating capacity of about 2,000—greater than that of New York's or Los Angeles' comedy clubs.*
>
> [Promoter] *Sue McLean says that "It surprises me every time we (sell out the 1,400-seat Guthrie) and add a second show for a Dana Carvey or Louie Anderson. The audience is huge." Promoter Kris Harvey-Stinson: "In the past, stand-up comedy was five minutes on Johnny Carson. But now there are scores of comedy specials on cable. That's proved it's a viable form of entertainment."*

"I think Seven Corners kept going more and more toward stand-up comedy," Dudley said, "while I was going more and more toward musical revues. Peter Tolan did some very good shows for me. So I thought I'd change it so you'd have a comedy revue on Hennepin and a musical revue at Seven Corners. They were very good shows, one of which got booked into New York. But it gets to be too much stuff."

And running two businesses eventually proved to be too much stuff for Dudley. He closed ETC in 1991 and consolidated his operations at 2605 South Hennepin.

The cast of the 1973 Brave New Workshop revue *In Search of a Cause; or, What's Left for the Left?* *Clockwise from left*: Doris Hess, Paul Menzel, Rochelle Richelieu and Michael McManus.

11

ON THE ROAD AND THE RADIO; OR, FROM GREECE TO CUBA AND INTO YOUR EAR

Did we say two businesses? You could safely call it at least three. Dudley had decided that his days of being a traveling showman were probably over, although he said that he was prepared to go back to the circus if he ever felt that the bloom had gone off the Brave New Workshop rose. That never came about—"Whenever I'd think I was done," he said, "something would happen that made me say, 'Oh, we really have to do a show about that'"—but that doesn't mean that he didn't still believe in the road as a good place to perform.

It wasn't long after the company's first revues that he assembled the first Brave New Workshop touring troupe, which would evangelize around the country, preaching the gospel of satire on college campuses and in small theaters.

"We started getting requests for graduation parties and schools, then going up to colleges to do a show in places like Moorhead [on Minnesota's western border]," Dudley recalled.

> *After about six months, they just took off, and all of a sudden, we had to have an extra company and an extra van. When it reached its peak, we had been doing colleges in forty states…So while the touring company was going out of town for three or four days a week, that ended up meaning that we needed more than one group to do it. And, eventually, we had them going out with the U.S. government to various places in a kind of USO* [United Service Organization] *situation* [which took them as far afield

as a 1965 trip to Greece]. *Those tours would go almost a month, and they'd all come back and quit.*

But there were a number of people who came up through touring and ended up on the main stage. So it always served that purpose, as well.

There were also shows elsewhere around town, like the annual performances at St. Paul's Macalester College in the early '60s or the very popular *The Art of Satire* at the Minneapolis Institute of Arts in 1964. (Dudley thought *The Satire of Art* would have been a more appropriate title.) A troupe would conclude the summer by doing a few shows a day at the Minnesota State Fair's Young America Center.

In 1977, the touring company did its first West Coast tour, but its peak may have been 1979, when it performed on 138 campuses in forty states. During that year, they came to the attention of the U.S. State Department, which booked the troupe to perform in Cuba, Puerto Rico and Panama in the summer of 1980. "And they haven't tried to censor it," Dudley said at the time. "Our subjects remain topical and broad enough so that Spanish-speaking members of the audience will understand." They also did a European USO tour the following year.

Back at home, as the Brave New Workshop was moving away from the scripted shows, improvisation acted as the sperm that fertilized the egg of an idea, the midwife that helped bring it into the world or played any number of roles in between. While Dudley had longed for improvisation to be more central to the company's process, it was Paul Menzel—freshly graduated from Carleton College in Northfield, Minnesota—who became the ally who ramped it up. Menzel helped teach the cast to create original material through improv.

However, it needed even more fresh energy to make it work, and some of it came in the person of Mark Keller. Keller said:

In 1971, I am a recent dropout from Yale Drama School, and I'm desperate to get into theater, but see no entry point anywhere. I'm back in Minneapolis from the East Coast because it's my hometown, and I really don't know where else to go or be. The Brave New Workshop is in the back of my mind, but I only knew of the place as being a venue for skits, funny songs and espresso. It wasn't taken seriously. I mean, I had friends working at the Guthrie at that point. Then I see a want ad that the Workshop is holding auditions for a training session, which might possibly end in a job. The idea was that you go see a show, and the audition would happen afterwards. So I went, more or less out of desperation, with no high expectations.

The show, Sigmund Freud's American Dream Machine, *blew me out of the water. It was clever, varied, the performers were terrific. I thought, "This is real theater! This isn't institutional crap; these folks are*

A promotional photo for *I'm OK, You're a Jerk: Changing the Lives of Millions,* a 1974 look at the pop psychology craze. *Left to right*: Doris Hess, Mark Keller, Neil Thompson (front), Michael McManus and Nancy Steen.

making their own theater! This is like Brecht, Moliere...the people who forged their plays themselves, for specific communities, developing topical material! Wow!" The director, Paul Menzel, asks me what I thought of the show, and I'm ready to pop.

After attracting relatively small crowds in the early '70s, attendance started picking up with 1973's *Ripped Off the Cross! The Last Crusade of Billy B'Jesus.* Keller said:

Finally, in late '73, "the cast" comes together: Neil Thompson, Michael McManus, Nancy Steen, Doris Hess and myself...What makes a cast "the cast?" Well, of course, talent. OK. Then, skill. Skill means you have experience in front of audiences. Comedy is a craft as much as an art, and even if you're talented, you need to learn the craft...But also, you don't have a strong cast unless the cast members are able to work together, to collaborate. They have to be stable, mature, respectful of each other, open to ideas, open to constructive criticism. This group had all of that. And then, bang, we had "the show." And that was the last show we all did together. It was called I'm OK, You're a Jerk, *derived from the title of the first monster self-help book of the era...And by this time, we're playing to solid sellout audiences every show, every night.*

In my opinion, this was when the Brave New Workshop came into its own. I stayed on for an additional five years after the rest of "the cast" left, and we did really great work, but all of it was laid on the foundation that had been put down by that group of actors and by Paul Menzel.

McManus wasn't quite the fresh-faced kid that the rest were; he'd come on board with his friend Pat Proft in the mid-'60s. But he remembers well the hard work that went into those '70s revues. McManus remembered:

We did nine shows a week and opened a new show every eight weeks or so. We still found three to four hours a day at least four days a week to develop new material through improvisation, which we then wrote and honed into a funny and often touching sketch. I think my '70s cast was more open to poignant slice-of-life material. And the cast was great.

Our best show was probably I'm OK, You're a Jerk *in early 1975... Mark, Neil Thompson and I did a long piece about three guys at a high school class reunion where they are the only ones who show up. In the piece, we find out they are the class dork, nerd and dweeb. It was very funny and touching. At the end, they hear laughter offstage and realize the whole thing was a set-up by the rest of the class to further humiliate them...It was a great show that got extended several times.*

At ETC (in 1972), I starred as Oscar Underwood in a political show that Proft originally did in the '60s, Yankee Doodle Dum Dum...*I*

Michael McManus portrays presidential candidate (and janitor) Oscar Underwood in the 1972 revue *Yankee Doodle Dum Dum.*

played an old janitor, so I whitened my hair, wore overalls, and carried a large push broom. To publicize the show, we did things like try to get Oscar on the presidential ballot in Minnesota. I appeared at the state fair with petitions or anywhere else to drum up business.

One time, I was sent to the state Democratic convention at the Leamington Hotel [in downtown Minneapolis] *in full costume. I was wandering around shaking hands when I noticed a gaggle of reporters surrounding someone important. Of course, I blundered right in and there was Senator* [Walter] *Mondale. Yikes. A short-ish lady newsperson from WCCO was trying her darnedest to reach in with her hand mike for Mondale's comment. She saw all 6'2" of me standing there and handed me her mike for my longer reach. I leaned way in and stuck the mike in Mondale's face. So here he is staring up at this huge guy with obviously powdered hair and dressed like a janitor, mike in one hand, broom in the other. He was a bit shaken by this specter of a crazed janitor/assassin but, being a good politician, hung in there anyway. I was not arrested.*

Did we say three businesses? Actually, there was another offshoot. In 1973, National Public Radio asked the Brave New Workshop to provide sketches built off the news for its relatively new afternoon news magazine, *All Things Considered.* It employed much of that same '70s cast to which Keller and McManus referred. Basically, the troupe was asked to come up with a topical collection of sketches and head into the studio to record them.

"My memories are that when we found out we were due to record more material, we just brainstormed and came up with timely stuff," McManus said.

It was usually more satirical than our stage work. If I had an idea, I'd write it and then whomever in the cast was appropriate to the sketch would perform it. Pretty simple. Nancy [Steen] *was great in these, as was Jim Cada. George Shea always came up with wonderful, bizarre pieces. He also was terrific in the studio.*

Neil Thompson and I did a series of pieces as two East Indian fellows (Sri and Baksa) who were always starving yet somehow commented on world events. The congressional committee that couldn't even order lunch without being entangled in parliamentary procedure was good. We even did a Charlie Chan bit about who was the culprit who turned up the thermostat during a power shortage.

Promiscuous Hostility and Laughs in the Land of Loons

The segments on *All Things Considered* turned out to be enormously popular, something that hit home with Brave New Workshop PR guy Mike Smith when he took a 1975 vacation in the northeast United States and decided to call up a few NPR affiliate stations and introduce himself. As he explained in a March 1975 *St. Paul Pioneer Press* story by Ozzie St. George soon thereafter, "I did interviews in Boston, Bangor, Buffalo and Philadelphia. The stations wanted to know all about the Workshop and the people who did the skits—who writes them, how we come up with them, how we got started."

In that article, St. George did a pretty good job of describing the process:

> *Since the Workshop is long on improvisational theater, a lot of the skits are improvised rather than written. Everybody contributes. Most of the skits run one to five minutes. They're topical, as noted. Usually, they're based on the month's "major news." The Arab oil embargo, for instance, triggered one—the ultimate embargo, called repossession. The Japanese came to this suburban home and seized the TV. The Italians took the shoes and the luggage. An Arab came and grabbed the (Arabic) house numbers... There was another one about a rooster—a rooster with a German or maybe a Russian accent—fouled up by the nation's sudden shift to (full-time) Daylight Savings Time a year ago* [implemented for energy-saving purposes]...
>
> *With skits in hand, 10 or 12 usually, parts are assigned. The Workshop company, luckily, has more voices than people and a good many dialects. Then, rehearsals. Then a day spent taping at Sound 80 Studios* [in Minneapolis's Seward neighborhood]. *These tapes are hustled off to Madison,* [Wisconsin,] *where Earplay* [which produced radio drama for NPR] *uses them to season* All Things Considered.
>
> *Nobody in radio does sound effects much anymore. So the Workshop company learned by doing.* [Director Paul] *Menzel still would like to find "a real old-time radio sound effects man," though. If there are any left.*

The segments were popular enough to inspire a 1975 record album called *Radio Comics*. It used sketches about which the troupe had received the most positive feedback, including that rooster sketch and one that McManus mentioned, "Point of Order," in which a congressional committee faces starvation because it can't cut back on bombastic rhetoric and clinging to parliamentary procedure long enough to agree on what kinds of sandwiches to order.

There was also "Breakout!" the story of a group of elderly nursing home residents who plot their escape from their drab confines, and "Electric

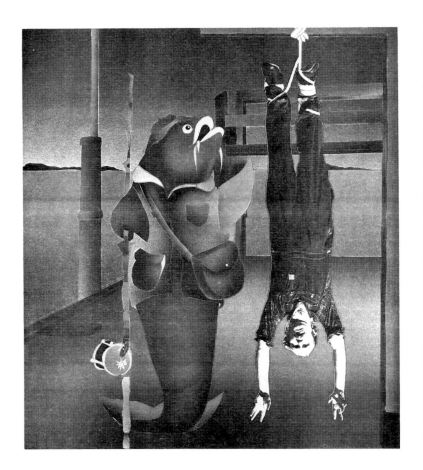

Scott Novotny getting hung up in the poster for 1979's *Upstream, Downstream: The World According to Carp*.

Medicine," in which a patient kept alive for years by multiple artificial organs finally succumbs, and the staff's sympathies are entirely with the machine that failed.

At this point, 160 stations around the country carried *All Things Considered*, and the relationship continued through the rest of the decade. But it's not like the Brave New Workshop wasn't also hot in its hometown. It was performing sketches on a light-hearted Sunday evening news magazine show on WCCO-TV called *Moore on Sunday* (under the title "Dudley Riggs' World in Revue"), and *Skyway News* referred to the company as "one of Minnesota's natural resources."

But there would be turnover in the cast. As McManus described it, "the two stages of working at the BNW: 1. What? You're paying me $75, and I get to do nine shows a week? Sweet! 2. What? You're paying me only $75, and I have to do nine shows a week? Shit!"

The poster for the 1977 revue *On a Clear Day, You Can See Your Mother.*

12

VIDEOSYNCRASIES;
OR, SEND IN THE CLONES

Here's theater writer Mike Steele in a February 1978 edition of the *Minneapolis Tribune*:

> *The workshop's brand of humor has traditionally been the verbal equivalent of dropping your pants—a fast, immediate laugh, the jokey smile, a relentlessly silly approach to reality, usually wrapped up with a four-letter expletive referring to bodily functions that sent the sea of adolescents which made up the workshop audience home happy and struck by the wonder of it all.*
>
> *But times change. The pimples vanish. Performers mature. The gods roar. The low humor of the workshop has been creeping up, first to the ankles, then the belt, occasionally moving toward the head and even the heart, comic still but nearer to real comedy, to real insights into real lives and real situations exploded by immediately identifiable fallibilities in the ever-funny human animal.*

Some very interesting things were afoot at 2605 South Hennepin. New artistic director Mark Keller helped create something that was more like a full-length play than anything the Workshop had previously offered. It was called *Uncle Sam is the Mother of Them All; or, Who Will Buy the Bicentennial?* It opened in the fall of 1975 and followed a semi-detached American everyman through American history from a New England whaling ship to a California gold field to a '50s classroom to being the last American out of Saigon at the fall.

And then there was the Monday Night Company. Just as the Brave New Workshop began as a way for Dudley to get people into his coffeehouse on slow Sunday nights, the Monday Night Company did the same thing for the following evening. But they ended up being an exceptionally talented crew that eventually formed the core of the touring company and the *All Things Considered* crew. Debuting in the summer of 1974, the Monday Company (or MOCO for short) soon gained its own following and became a transitional troupe between improv workshops or classes and the main-stage company.

There was turnover, and a mostly new Monday Night Company cast made a splash with shows that reflected the economic tenor of the times, like 1975's *Selling Out; or, Big Brother Can You Spare Some Change?* and 1976's *The Recession Follies* (a title revived in 1992; economic downturns are gifts that keep on giving). Critics praised *Selling Out* for clever skits like Mesopotamians trying to put the *X* back in Xmas, Mrs. Lazarus demanding a refund on her husband's funeral and two ducks meeting while flying south and sharing battle stories: "I was with a flight of mallards out of Winnipeg and got caught in a firefight a few miles back."

But the main-stage productions at 2605 were also lauded. Peter Vaughan of the *Minneapolis Star* said of *Today Is the Last Day of Your Life, So Far* (1976) that "it is evident the workshop has come of age." It was a somewhat dark and cynical show that included a memorable skit about three failed suicides commiserating, one of whom tried to feed himself to piranhas and found that they'd lost their teeth to a disease. Now he's covered with piranha hickeys.

Similarly, Don Morrison of the *Star* said of 1977's *Rich Dope, Poor Dope*: "Their material is happy proof that the Workshop has finally grown up and away from the noisy, thumb-in-the-eye sarcasms that often passed for satire in its earlier days." One of its most popular sketches was built around a couple that takes the phone off the hook in order to have some privacy during a tryst and ends up encountering anxious operators, police helicopters and a suicidal mother.

That same year, *I Hear What You're Saying, but I Don't Care* featured an absurd interlude in which Susan Fuller was carried onstage while singing an operatic aria and continued to do so while John Stinson tried to distract her before finally giving up and carrying her off while she continued to sing. As Vaughan said in his *Star* review, "there seemed to be little obvious point to the exercise, but its pure lunacy was a delight."

"There was a man who attended every Dudley show at least three times," Fuller said.

The cast of 1980's *Dork at the Top of the Stairs*. *Left to right:* John Wehrman, Scott Novotny, Leslie Curtin and Peggy Knapp.

His name was Stuart, and if he liked your sketch, he laughed harder than anyone else in the audience. The problem was that his laugh was this high-pitched, out-of-breath giggle. We were always told before the show if Stuart was in the audience, because he not only cracked up the audience, he cracked us up onstage. We thought we nearly lost him during some particularly funny sketches—he would be gasping for air.

By this time, the Riggs crew was presenting comedy revues, plays, musical revues, radio sketches and TV segments. So how about film? That came into play when John Remington was artistic director from 1978 to '84. Remington said:

Bringing multimedia, film, video, interactive play into the shows was the newest and biggest development in the shows we did during my tenure as artistic director. My first show, Nitwork; or, Send in the Clones, *was totally held together with this multimedia integration…I also produced, wrote and directed eight film shorts, using actors from the company. They were used in the shows but also entered into film festivals. They all made it as finalists in the American Film Festival*

Grant Wood's painting *American Gothic* inspired a few different Brave New Workshop posters, including for this 1983 revue about the advance of technology.

and got some showings on Showtime and HBO, when they were so new, they were hungry for content.

It wasn't always an easy transition: While creating *Nitwork*, the company threw out a month's worth of material because they felt that the technological aspects were taking over the show. But critics took notice of the change and found it refreshing. Don Morrison of the *Star* noted that local TV news anchor Ron Magers taped some spoofs that were broadcast on the newly installed TV monitors on either side of the stage. But Morrison especially liked a scene in which live action and video interacted.

There is deliciously spooky wit in one of the numbers involving a bank's instant-cash machine with a closed-circuit TV camera and screen in which a customer can see himself. As the poor boob is punching buttons, he suddenly notices on the screen that wild things are happening behind him. But, when he turns around, there's nothing to be seen. A beautifully synchronized interplay between the live actor and crazy happenings on the monitor reduces our hapless fellow to nervous collapse.

Yes, the Brave New Workshop was using technology to criticize technology's place in our lives. For example, in 1982's *Videosyncrasies; or, Rich Man, Pac-Man*, a fourteen-year-old's parents forbid him from playing his beloved *Pac-Man* video game ("It's family day. We're all going to have fun and clean the basement!"). So he responds by turning the voracious yellow Pac-Man loose on his household and neighborhood.

And the place of the computer in our lives was imaginatively satirized in 1983's *I Compute, Therefore IBM*. *Star Tribune* critic Mike Steele had a prescient description:

The computer as icon, data as holy writ, computing as the road to salvation; the Riggs troupe wants to take a large byte out of our humanist misconceptions. The Vatican may be in Rome, but Control Data, the modern mother church, is right here. We're a post-cathedral community. Technology is the New Wave faith. The workshop's latest show asks the question, "Have you accepted a personal computer into your life?"

That revue opened with a video feed to the actors' green room in which cast members receive word that they've all been fired. After they leave, Dudley walks in with his "Acme Actron Kit with Comedy Module," starts it up and creates four new actors who look just like the four who are freshly unemployed. The actors then appear on stage and begin the show.

Peter Tolan was an actor, writer, director, composer and music director at Brave New Workshop and ETC who created original musical revues at ETC in the 1980s. He's now an Emmy-winning TV writer and producer.

13

YOUR REVIEW OF REVUES;
OR, SIDE BY SIDE BY SODOM

Avenue for musical revues. That was Dudley's vision for ETC before stand-up comedy became the big draw. And his years as an impresario (not to mention growing up in the circus) had taught him that you go where there's an audience. But he needed someone who shared that vision, who would have the energy and imagination to bring those musical revues to pass.

Along came Peter Tolan.

"I was actively flunking out of the University of Massachusetts around the spring of 1980," Tolan said.

I worked as a house manager for the campus's two-thousand-seat Fine Arts Center, and a great Falstaffian Scotsman was the head of the backstage crew. His name was Jim MacRostie, and he was with Dudley at the very beginning. I had written and produced a series of very successful on-campus musical revues—very topical stuff—and when I told Mac my career as a student at UMass was going belly-up, he said, "You should work for this theater in Minneapolis I was associated with." That was the first time I heard about the Brave New Workshop. He took me up to his office and called Dudley and put us on the phone together. It was a brief conversation, and then Mac took the phone and said, "Peter's a clever young fellow and you should give him a job." Dudley said he would hire me. I was amazed! I'd been warned that a life in the theater would be a constant struggle, but there I sat—suddenly employed, and with zero effort on my part!

I screwed around in my hometown of Scituate, Massachusetts, for the summer, then made my way west by train...When I got to Minneapolis, I told the cab driver to take me to Dudley Riggs'. Luckily, he took me to the ETC at Seven Corners because that's where Dudley was that evening. It was like a scene from a movie: me walking up to the door of the theater in the rain, two suitcases containing most of my earthly possessions in hand. I had arrived for my job in the theater, and within a very short time, I found out exactly what that job was: I would be the janitor at the Brave New Workshop.

So much for a life in the theater without struggle.

But Tolan was only the janitor for about a month. Tolan continued:

I guess the Brave New Workshop people knew I could play the piano because some months later they called and said they needed a new music director for the touring company. I'm not an accomplished player, but I was good enough to get the job done. During that time, I started taking improv classes at the theater. I was pretty quick on my feet and enjoyed the sound of my own voice, so I really took to improv. And I guess I made an impression on the powers that were at the time, because after a few more months, I was made a member of the main company at the BNW.

Among the shows in which he performed was 1982's *May the Force of Habit Be with You,* which examined traditions and our adherence to them. It contained a lengthy sketch about a daughter who decides to make fettuccine Alfredo for Christmas dinner, and it still merits a mention whenever a Brave New Workshop crew begins brainstorming for one of their (extremely popular) Christmas shows today.

Tolan recalled:

One of the bits in that sketch was the mother [Vicki Dakil] *playing her beloved album of* Ethel Merman's Greatest Christmas Hits. *That came about because, during rehearsals, I would do this truly awful Ethel Merman imitation—it was mostly screeching with a wild, unpredictable vibrato—and our director, John Remington, thought it was funny. So I recorded several tracks for the album one night with* [music director] *Raymond Berg, and I can honestly say that recording session was the closest I've come in my adult life to wetting my pants. It got so crazy, John decided I should do a short sketch as Merman, which would appear earlier in the show before the Christmas sketch. Sort of foaming the runway, I guess. It was basically me, in full drag, screaming at the audience for two minutes. I'd start out with recognizable Merman hits, then she'd get a little crazy and start singing "I Am the Walrus." It was insanity—but how to end it? So I'm singing—and [Chris] Denton comes out riding a chair like it's a car. And you're hearing the engine noise being supplied by Steve Rentfrow in the booth. And he gets to center stage behind me—and the engine goes dead. He tries to start the car a couple times. No go. So he gets up and pulls out jumper cables and attaches them to my tits and restarts the car. He drives off—end of sketch. Lunacy.*

Peggy Knapp was a member of that cast. She said:

Peter as Merman sang with a voice that rattled the rafters, took the enamel off your teeth and sent rats fleeing into the alley.

Peter once wrote a spoof of the song "The Wreck of the Edmund Fitzgerald" that was hilarious. It began: The day it was hot, when they took out the yacht/That belonged to Muffy and Harold./With their tonics and gins, and their caviar in tins/And the records of Ella Fitzgerald…

Working with Peter gave me the confidence to stand up and sing in front of an audience. He had so much fun doing music, it spread to the rest of the cast and made us brave.

Oh, by the way, *May the Force of Habit Be with You* won a Kudos Award from the Twin Cities Drama Critics Circle as one of the best productions of 1982.

After four Brave New Workshop revues, Tolan moved over to ETC to create original revues with an emphasis on the music. The first was *Altered Stages*, a collaboration with Joel Gelpe. In a preview article, Mike Steele of the *Minneapolis Tribune* described it thus:

The subject of the revue will be Twin Cities Theater itself—you know Twin Cities theater: more theaters per capita than any city since Periclean Athens, more stand-up comics than bus shelters, every third person a budding playwright. That *Twin Cities theater.*

Tolan and Gelpe spoofed the Guthrie in a sketch in which artistic director Liviu Ciulei is forced to do nothing but Neil Simon; Children's Theatre Company (with a commission from the Catholic Church) combining the life of Jesus and Babar in "500 Pounds of Faith"; Chanhassen Dinner Theatres inspiring a woman who now eats at every theater she attends; Theatre de la

Jeune Lune doing a show about a clown out of work during the depression; and an arena-style stab at ETC's neighbor, Theatre in the Round Players.

In the summer of 1983, Tolan staged the final incarnation of *Miss America*, pairing it with a one-act original musical revue and calling it *Miss America and Her First Act*. It sold out its entire run at ETC, so Tolan took that momentum and created his first evening-length revue for which he wrote both book and music, *Les Follies Bourgeois; or, Can the Middle Class Can-Can?* It featured that aforementioned Lake Minnetonka boat ballad; a Reagan appreciation to "This Old Man"; a Scandinavian family becoming instantly Jewish when visiting the Lincoln Del restaurant; an Irving Berlin version of *Cats*; a religious treatment of designer fashions incorporating a gospel tune; a look at the "me" generation entitled "Marching for Apathy"; a couple from Iowa visiting their favorite Minneapolis hotel, restaurant and bank and finding only craters; and a one-man, six-minute version of *The Wizard of Oz*.

In a *Minneapolis Star Tribune* story around that time, Tolan said, "I've talked to Dudley about doing more musical satire. It would be good and I think the ETC needs some kind of identity. I'm just not sure that I can keep turning them out like rabbits."

But turn them out he did. Tolan notes that his casts grew progressively smaller. *Miss America and Her First Act* employed eight, *Les Follies Bourgeois* four and *First Times, Second Thoughts* was a two-hander performed by Tolan and Linda Wallem, another veteran of the Brave New Workshop who came on board after Tolan's departure from the South Hennepin space.

Of *First Times, Second Thoughts*, Tolan said, "I remember Act Two started with a very long parody of *A Prairie Home Companion*, which was big at the time. I did a fairly good Garrison Keillor impression, but I don't think the sketch was super solid. I think, more than anything, I was just showing off the impression."

Then there was, as Tolan calls it, "a full-blown musical" in *Hang On to This!; or, Night of the Living Bread*—"quite obviously inspired by the success and structure of *Little Shop of Horrors*"—and a play with music about a reunion of old friends, *Breakfast at Chappaquiddick*.

But then Tolan moved on. On September 4, 1984, four years to the day after he arrived, suitcases in hand, he lit off for New York. But Twin Cities director Sandy Hey did ask him to create a new revue for ETC in 1987, and he responded with *Fixing Men: A Woman's Guide to Home Repair*. Tolan said, "I remember an extended sketch based on the idea of how different the world would be if men were the ones who had a menstrual cycle. I know there was congressional action taken immediately to find a cure!" It was a hit that was extended and inspired a revised revival the following year that featured a memorable spoof of a Gilbert and Sullivan operetta called "Fertilization," in which three sperm cells dressed as Victorian Italian sailors struggle toward their goal, an egg.

Tolan's final visit to ETC came in 1988, when he and Wallem tried out their new revue *One Hour and Forty-Five Minutes from Broadway* before performing it at an off-Broadway theater in New York. It featured some of Tolan's patented offbeat musical theater hybrids, like Gilbert and Sullivan with Sam Shepard sitting in for Gilbert, *Cabaret*'s Kander and Ebb doing *The Iliad*, Stephen Sondheim adapting *Fun with Dick and Jane* and Irving Berlin doing Franz Kafka's *Metamorphosis*.

In order to enter the "house" of the theater at 2605 South Hennepin Avenue, one passes through a kind of hall of fame that displays posters from Brave New Workshop's history.

14

TECH TROUBLE WITH STEVIE RAY; OR, WHAT COULD POSSIBLY GO WRONG?

It was the Brave New Workshop that set Steve Rentfrow on his career path when he saw a touring company perform at Moorhead State University (now known as Minnesota State–Moorhead) while he was a student there. He created his own degree program called "Theory and Performance of Comedy" and, after graduating in 1983, headed to the Twin Cities and started taking improv classes.

He ended up playing a major role in the company, but not as an actor. Yes, he was with the touring company for a little while, but his biggest impact came when he was hired as technical director, first for the touring company and then at ETC and, finally, at 2605 South Hennepin. Eventually, Rentfrow left to start his own comedy theater and improv school under the "Stevie Ray's" banner. Two of his students were Jenni Lilledahl and John Sweeney, but we'll get to their stories in a little while. First, we should give you a sense of what it was like to handle the lights, sound and sets for Brave New Workshop shows, at least back in the day.

The first monster that Rentfrow had to wrestle was the board that controlled the stage lighting at ETC. Here's how he remembered it:

> *The board was so old—the manufacturer went out of business 20 years earlier—that some of the metal contacts under the sliders were wearing thin. If you slid the control to the wrong spot, sparks would emit from the board and the lights would flash. I mentioned this to Tom Loddengaard, who oversaw the space at ETC, and he asked Dudley about it. Dudley, always saving a dollar, was actually able to find replacement parts from a lighting graveyard across the*

country. Tom kept after Dudley, letting him know that there were newfangled boards with master controls and even computer pre-sets!...One day, when Tom was working once again to fix the board, a huge jolt came through the metal casing, sending Tom flying out of the booth. He landed on the floor right at Dudley's feet. Dudley looked down at Tom and calmly said, "You can buy a new light board now."

And then there was the balloon drop. Rentfrow said:

Like most other theaters, the Brave New Workshop and ETC had special celebrations for New Year's Eve. While I was tech director at the ETC, we tried to devise fun ways to add flair while staying within the budget—which was less than most people spend on a child's birthday party. The ETC theater had a very high ceiling, so we wanted a balloon drop and flying confetti. For a balloon drop, we got large nets and stapled them to the ceiling. We laced a small rope through the mesh of the nets and ran it to the booth. When I would pull the cord, the nets would part and the balloons would drop.

For a confetti machine, I found a small desk fan in the basement and mounted it on a platform so it would face upwards. I constructed a huge cardboard funnel above the fan so when confetti dropped through the funnel it would hit the fan and fly in all directions. I mounted the entire contraption on the ceiling in the center of the theater. The funnel had a flap that opened and closed using a rope from the tech booth. I ran an extension cord from the fan to the booth. When I plugged in the fan and pulled the rope to open the flap, voila! Confetti!

One of the ETC employees was asked to blow up balloons for a couple of days leading up to New Year's Eve. She decided to speed up the process by using the CO2 tank for the soft drink dispenser. She slipped the balloon over the nozzle and shot CO2 gas to fill up the balloon. I spent a week in the tech booth during shows cutting up confetti. I used scissors to cut up old newspapers into tiny confetti. The big night came and we loaded the confetti machine and the balloon nets. Then we waited during two sold-out shows to release chaos onto the audience.

At about midway through the second show, we realized our first mistake. Air typically leaks through the skin of a balloon over a week or so. CO2 gas is thinner than air, so it leaks faster. Throughout the second show of the night, the balloons were all growing smaller and smaller; so small that they started to fall through the nets on the ceiling. Audience members would occasionally have a tiny balloon drop onto their lap for no reason. Also, when small chunks of newspaper are put in a pile, as in the giant funnel I built, the paper compresses and sticks together. So, when the time came for the balloon and confetti drop, what balloons were still remaining in the nets dropped like little rubber blobs. When I turned on the fan and opened the flap, a small handful of confetti dropped out; that's it. I yanked on the rope to open and close the flap, hoping to loosen the confetti. No luck.

So our audience was treated to small rubber blobs and the feeling that someone tossed a handful of newspaper flakes on them. After the audience emptied the theater, I stood underneath the confetti machine with a long pole and poked at the newspaper confetti through the flap. All of a sudden, there was a rush of confetti on my head, plus where ever the fan spread the rest. I spent the rest of the night sweeping up confetti that took two weeks to cut, and that no one else saw. Happy New Year's! The next year, we just handed out noise makers.

Not all the technical elements of a Brave New Workshop show were so seat-of-the-pants. As mentioned earlier, audiences and critics were quite impressed with how effectively the company was using video in its shows. However, putting those videos together sometimes caused problems. Rentfrow said:

For Bomb Voyage; or, Desperately Leaking Fusion *in 1986, we needed to videotape a segment in a nearby field. The entire cast showed up, and I brought the video camera from the theater. This was in an urban field with houses nearby, but some weird guy kept riding his bike near us to see what was going on. After a while, he came over and asked, "Whatcha guys doin'? Makin' a movie?" We brushed him off as politely as we could, but we were still a bit creeped out at a guy in his thirties on a bike in the middle of the afternoon. So he hovered nearby to watch. After we set everything up, we discovered that the camera battery was dead. I think it was the tech director's job to charge it up, whoever that was. We are standing there without a clue as to what to do. A dead battery, out in the middle of a field, and the clock is ticking.*

The next thing we know, the weird guy walks up and asks, "What's wrong?"

Not wanting to get any more involved with him than we already were, we quickly said, "The camera battery is dead."

He asked, "Can you plug the camera into an outlet?"

We thought, "What a dolt! There isn't an outlet within one hundred yards." Instead, we said, "Yeah, but we're kind of stuck out here."

Without hesitation, he said, "I'll be right back. Wait here."

He rode off on his bike and came back in a truck. He opened the tailgate and pulled out a gas-powered generator. He parked about fifty feet away so the noise wouldn't ruin the shoot. He fired up the generator, pulled out a fifty-foot extension cord and plugged us in.

The cast of *Dork at the Top of the Stairs* hits one of Minneapolis's lakeside trails in the summer of 1980. *Left to right*: John Wehrman, Cliff Walinski, Scott Novotny, Leslie Curtin and Peggy Knapp.

So we got the shoot done just right and on time, the weird guy turned out to be smarter than the rest of us, and I went home to a nice helping of humble pie.

And then there was the heat, which was frequently an issue at summer shows at the theater on South Hennepin Avenue. Rentfrow said:

Sold-out shows meant a lot of bodies putting out BTUs. The only air conditioning was a window unit that was so loud it could only be run during intermission. There was another building AC unit in the basement, but it was so old that it cooled the air by running water over wooden slats with a big fan…But eventually that old beast died. Dudley couldn't afford ceiling fans, so I had to buy six window fans and run conduit wire across the ceiling for outlets. Each fan was angled so the air was pushed to the next fan in a big circle. I installed a motor control in the tech booth so I could have the fans at any speed we needed. During intermission, we cranked those babies up to full speed and the entire theater became a vortex. We discovered something interesting: moving hot air in a big circle doesn't make it cooler.

If it wasn't heat, it was rain.

Since Dudley never actually owned the Brave New Workshop space in Uptown, he was at the whim of the landlord when it came to minor issues, such as a leaky roof. At one point, it was raining so hard that we had to ask a few audience members to hold buckets in their laps during the show. Being true Minnesotans, they took it all in good fun. It was either that or not see the show. I learned quickly to put a towel in the bucket or we would hear plunk, plunk, plunk *throughout the show. The lobby and hallway to the theater were so bad it was like walking under a waterfall. I had to nail massive sheets of plastic across the entire ceiling. I cut one hole in the lowest part of the tarp so all the water would run to that spot. I glued a rubber hose around the hole and ran the hose to a large metal garbage can. We would empty the garbage can before the show, at intermission and after the show. Each time, the garbage can was completely full; which meant we were getting about forty gallons of water through the ceiling per hour. The new theater downtown lacks a certain charm by being dry all the time.*

While modern tech crews tend to communicate via headsets, there was more of a "One if by land, two if by sea" way of doing things at 2605 Hennepin. Rentfrow explained:

In the old days, in order to start the show, we needed to know that the actors were ready. As I sat in the tech booth, I would typically try to wave at Drew Jansen, the music director. He had a small hole in the wall between his booth and backstage. He would check with the actors and then wave back, then I could start the show. Sometimes this system broke down because it was difficult to see each other or communicate effectively. I would dim the lights to start the show, only to find out there was an issue I was not aware of and we would have to start over. We couldn't install a voice intercom because the music booth was open to the audience.

So I wired a small box between the music and tech booths with three small LED lights on each—red, yellow and green—with corresponding colored switches. When you flipped a switch on your light box, that color LED would flash in the other person's booth. If I flashed green to Drew and he flashed green in response, the show was ready to start. If he flashed red in response, I would wait until I saw green. Smooth…Drew and I developed an extensive communication system with the LED boxes. For instance, three green flashes meant, "That was funny!" Two reds and a yellow meant, "What is up

The cast of 1985's *All Stressed up with No Place to Go* portraying allegorical characters that represent several sources of stress. *Left to right*: Beth Gilleland, Dane Stauffer, Jim Detmar, Linda Wallem and Peter Staloch.

with this audience?" In our time at Dudley Riggs, we had dozens of full-on conversations during the show without ever uttering a sound.

And then there was "Grandpa's Head."

In 1986, during the writing of The Viceman Cometh, *Dane Stauffer came to me and said, "Steve, I need you to make a box that looks like an old steamer trunk. I need to be able to sit in it with my head sticking out, and there needs to be a bunch of wires so it looks like the box is keeping my head alive." When you worked with Dane, you got accustomed to this kind of conversation. Apparently, he came up with a sketch idea, "Grandpa's Head," that involved an old vaudeville performer gradually having his body go bad until his head was being kept alive by a machine. Being an aging performer, he chose to have the machine put inside his old steamer trunk so he could remember his days on the road.*

The cast of 1985's *All Stressed up with No Place to Go* engages in some stress reduction. *Left to right*: Peter Staloch, Linda Wallem, Jim Detmar, Dane Stauffer and Beth Gilleland.

What I ended up with was a plywood box painted black, with metal strips and rivets attached to make it look like a steamer trunk. Dane could sit inside and push himself with his feet through a hidden opening in the bottom…It took over a month to build. I also found an electronic roulette game at Radio Shack where you pushed a button and LED lights flashed around a circular board until they stopped on a number. I removed the switch so the lights spun continuously. When you opened the "service panel" on the steamer trunk, you saw these flashing lights spinning, plus wires and clear plastic tubes filled with "blood." I also connected wires to the LED ports on the circuit board and strung them to the sides of the box. I drilled tiny holes and inserted red LEDs; the holes were drilled in the pattern of a cardiac rhythm. When Dane hit a switch inside the box, the audience literally saw his heartbeat pattern flashing on the box. When Grandpa died at the end of the sketch, he "danced" around the stage in the box to dream music created by Drew Jansen, slowly stopping and turning off the lights. It was one of the goofiest death scenes in the theater, yet the audience still got teary-eyed when he finally passed away.

Because the hole for the head was built for someone only Dane's height, no one else could ever understudy as Grandpa's head; Dane never missed a show. After the show closed, Dudley wanted us to place the "Grandpa's Head" box in the lobby and charge people "a dollar a head" to have their picture taken. For the rest of my time at Dudley Riggs, anytime Dane said, "Steve, I have a neat idea," I ran in the opposite direction.

The graying of America was addressed in a 1982 revue.

15

DON'T PANIC, NO ONE'S IN CONTROL; OR, THE MAN WHO SHOT LIBERAL VALUES

S econd City cheats.

OK, there's always been something of a friendly rivalry between the Brave New Workshop and Chicago's more famous company, the Second City. The Brave New Workshop likes to point out that it's America's longest continuously running comedy theater, even though the Second City could legitimately make the same claim, as it was founded in 1959, and Dudley—despite presenting comedy of one sort or another at Café Espresso starting in 1958—didn't officially launch the Brave New Workshop until 1961.

But, when she started studying at the Second City in the early '80s, Sue Scott was surprised the first time she did a live improv show there.

> *At Second City—and I don't know if it's the case now, but it certainly was then—they would take suggestions from the audience and then they'd go backstage and say, "You know that sketch we're working on for the next show about the fireman and his family? Let's just change it to a policeman and do that." And I was interning and taking classes, and I'd see this and say, "What? That's cheating! That's not instant theater!" It was their way of fine-tuning and honing scripts for the next show.*
>
> *Then I got to Dudley Riggs, and they don't do that. It's instant. And I was thinking, "Oh, Dudley Riggs is so much better than Second City, even though they're the second cousin and in Minneapolis instead of big old bad Chicago." So I was so pleased that I was able to get in with the*

true practitioners of improvisation instead of this hybrid, well-we-fake-it-a-bit, pay-no-attention-to-the-man-behind-the-curtain kind of thing.

Yes, but those are just the improv sets. In fairness, both companies use improvisation as a means toward creating their revues, using some tools that are very similar, some not. Sue Scott was a Brave New Workshop cast member in 1983 and '84 who has gone on to be a member of the cast of Garrison Keillor's weekly radio program, *A Prairie Home Companion*, portraying most of the female characters heard on it since 1992. Here's how she describes how improv was used to create a show in her days at the Brave New Workshop:

> *When you worked there, you didn't do anything else except laundry on Monday. I'd run into people and they'd say, "Hey, where ya been?" and I'd say, "I'm at Dudley Riggs." We'd be there every day Tuesday through Saturday for five- to seven-hour sessions. Sometimes we'd develop the theme for the next show, sometimes it was one that Dudley really wanted us to tackle. Or the timing would dictate it, like, for example, I was with the company as we crossed over into 1984. That was just a no-brainer theme, that we had to touch on all of that Orwellian stuff.*
>
> *Then, once the show had opened, that next Tuesday, we would start meeting to write the next show. If we already had a theme, we would brainstorm a title, "How about this? How about this?" We'd laugh a lot. And we literally could be in the theater for two days or two and a half coming up with a title. Because the titles were crucial. And some of those titles were pieces of art in and of themselves. So clever and biting and satirical.*
>
> *And then we'd start brainstorming sketch ideas, and we'd jump up onstage and start improvising some of them. And then, if something seemed like a funny idea, it would get assigned. "Why don't you two guys go and write that? Or why don't you go and flesh that out a little what we just did?" So it was all incredibly collaborative in the creation of the sketches, but the fine tuning would be assigned to particular people. "You have a handle on that sketch better than anyone else. Why don't you take what we did today and write it out?" And then we would write it out in script form.*

And it wasn't just about what would be funny.

"The core group that I was in was so determined that not everything in the show should be funny. There should be something that's poignant,

The political bent that's been part of Brave New Workshop shows since the beginning was still a major source of inspiration in 1983.

something that could be meaningful, touching. So we really embraced those moments, too."

For example, Scott wrote and performed an extended monologue about a woman expressing her worries about what she could personally do to keep nuclear war from happening. There was also an extended playlet that portrayed some sibling relationships in all of their tenderness and prickliness. Scott said:

> *Then, you'd create the shows and do them, and every night there would be an improv set. That's where the rubber meets the road. You're out there, naked in front of everybody and it either works or it doesn't. It soars. It bombs. Improv training is the best training for anyone in any field. Because of that whole "Yes, and…" idea of building on things in a positive way. Don't edit. All of those things we learn are so valuable. Go with the impulse. They're all great ideas for how to live your life. But improv? Things don't get scarier or more exhilarating. "All right, we're going to make something out of nothing, and not only is it going to be something, it's going to be a whole package wrapped up with a bow and it is going to be hi-fricking-larious. But no pressure…"*
>
> *Now how could that training not be good for lawyers, ministers, politicians, doctors, nurses…? Anyone who has to get in front of people.*

For her four shows with the Brave New Workshop, Scott was one of two women in the cast, the other being Beth Gilleland. Together, they created memorable sketches like "For White Girls Who Have Considered Analysis When Electrolysis is Enuf," in which, as the *Star Tribune*'s Mike Steele said, they examined "the name-brand, peer pressure psyches of the white upper-middle class with something close to Dada zaniness." That was in 1984's *Don't Panic, No One's in Control*, a revue that concluded with teachers being forced to perform the specialties they're teaching for merit pay. (Steele: "You can pick out teachers in the audience by the level of groans and pain.")

All of the BNW cast and artistic leadership turned over after that revue, except for Gilleland, who stayed for another year. By that time, she'd already become a critics' darling, Steele saying in a review of 1983's *Nitwork II, the Sequel; or, Don't Bother, the Clones are Here*: "Gilleland is slowly creating a personal style that might end up being the funniest ever at the Workshop." But she truly hit her stride in the mid-'80s cast. She said:

Richard Guindon isn't as well known in the Twin Cities for being a co-founder of Brave New Workshop as he is for his *Minneapolis Tribune* cartoons. Here, his professional identities merge on a 1985 poster.

I have fondness for all of the shows I worked on, but I remember Yuppie See, Yuppie Do *as being particularly topical and successful. It ran for seven months straight without a break. We had a tight harmony Manhattan Transfer opening. "Don't you see…it's mostly me…and hardly ever…you." We all wore shirts with ties. Jim Detmar and I had a recurring sketch about a couple so concerned about their professional lives that they couldn't make a commitment in their personal relationship. The cast was tight—Linda Wallem, me, Jim Detmar, Peter Staloch and Dane Stauffer—and it was a blast to perform together.*

I still enjoy the lyrics to "Math Anxiety," a song I wrote with Peggy Knapp and Raymond Berg for I Compute, Therefore IBM. *"While the boys were taking woodshop/we learned to put in darts./ Good god don't take geometry/'cause you ain't got the smarts./They were making cedar chests/while we were sitting pretty./They cut angles, we cut cake,/now we're sitting shitty." It was lovely to work on a song that addressed a female concern.*

Yuppie See, Yuppie Do; or, Bye Buy American (1985) featured an Old West political allegory in which a gunslinger named Liberal Values (as opposed to "Liberty Valance" from a classic western) arrives in Trickle Down Gulch and confronts the new sheriff who's taking away food stamps. The sheriff would shoot him if it weren't for the intervention of the private schoolmarm. ("There are no more public schools, Liberal.") He slowly leaves town, saying he'll come back when he comes up with some new ideas.

Many special partnerships have developed on the Brave New Workshop stage over the decades, and one was that of Gilleland and Dane Stauffer. Longtime Workshop visitors still talk of the punky pair they played in the Thornton Wilder send-up "Our Uptown," from 1984's *Time Is On My Side…And I'm Having It Removed.*

Dane Stauffer said, "What an extraordinary company we had. *Yuppie See, Yuppie Do* was a huge hit. *All Stressed up with No Place to Go* topped it. 'The Stuckey's Mystery'"—in which two robbers with limps hold up Stuckey's restaurants on a stormy night and all of the characters end up gathered at a Stuckey's, all with limps, all menacing—"Peter Staloch's 'Cow Song,' 'Monty's Meat and Music,' a fun Danny Kaye–ish romp and [1987's] *The Viceman Cometh* has, I think, my favorite all-time sketch: 'Grandpa's Head.'"

He also made a strong impression with audiences in *Time Is On My Side* as, according to Steele, "a modern, curiosity-crazed kid who can't sleep because

Beth Gilleland and Dane Stauffer developed a chemistry in Brave New Workshop revues that led to original two-person shows like *Shedding Light All Over Your Good Black Skirt*.

he's worried about things like metaphysics, infinity, eternity and what happens to matter, though on a boyish level. After discussing molecules, he can't sleep because he realizes his bed could have been a person."

Together, Gilleland and Stauffer created a two-person show called *Shedding Light All Over Your Good Black Skirt* that they premiered at ETC and took to Scotland's prestigious Edinburgh Festival.

Stauffer said:

> *When I determined it was time to leave (which I hated to do, but felt a "time to move on" feeling), I proposed to Dudley an idea for a one-man show. He let me develop* Duesenberg 55 *at the ETC on Tuesday nights. I got solid reviews, got accepted into the Playwrights' Center on a Jerome [Foundation] Fellowship, and the show got picked up by other theaters.*
>
> *I remember going into Dudley's "office" in the ETC (a little room filled with all sorts of…intriguing piles of…intrigue) and reading him my ten-page pitch. He paused and then said, "I think it is funny, it has a point of*

Among the cast of 1988's *Safer Than Sex* were (*left to right*) Michelle Cassioppi, Peter Staloch, Christine Decker and Gene Larche.

view, and it is a perfect growth opportunity for you. Let's do it!"
Dudley was a big supporter and mentor for me and still is.

Oh, and…There was one more writer who made a big difference at the Brave New Workshop in the late '80s. According to cast member Greg Triggs, "when Lorna Landvik joined the company, the writing went through the roof." He particularly remembered

a charming sketch about a nursing home on New Year's Eve. Michelle Hutchinson was an attendant stuck with all these old people. Lorna's character had dementia and thought she was a Cotton Club—era horn player. I was her boyfriend, Mr. Bartlett, a retired lit professor who only spoke in recognizable quotes. It was beautiful—funny, good satire, sentimental without losing its point of view.

Triggs also fondly remembers the holiday shows like *Not a Christmas Carol*. "Super fun stuff," he recalled. "*Rudolph the Red Nosed Reindeer* meets *Dallas/Dynasty*. Really fun 'Mrs. Claus' song where Mark Copenhaver, Melissa Denton and I played horny little elves to Mo Collins and Michelle Hutchinson's Mrs. C."

A musically inclined (or not) promotional photo for 1985's *All Stressed up with No Place to Go*, featuring (*left to right*) Jim Detmar, Linda Wallem, Peter Staloch and Dane Stauffer.

16

BRAVE NEW WORKSHOP'S GREATEST HITS; OR, THE PIRATES OF PENNZOIL

S ongs have been a part of the Brave New Workshop's revues ever since the first cast took the stage in 1961 to the tune of "Happy Days Are Here Again" ("in an arrangement just cheerful enough to be ironic," company member Michael Anthony recalled in a 1983 *Minneapolis Tribune* article). While some of the songs from Brave New Workshop revues have taken tunes from elsewhere and supplied them with new lyrics, the best ones are the totally original creations. Here are some of the songs that Workshop performers, critics and audiences have found particularly memorable:

"Herman" (1962)
The song that helped put Brave New Workshop on the map. Written by Dan Sullivan and debuted by Ruth Williams at the Miss St. Paul pageant, it was reprised on the 1963 *Miss America* album.

"Mr. Skrowaczewski" (1963)
Terry Erkkala wrote this song of lusty longing for Minneapolis Symphony music director Stanislaw Skrowaczewski, begging the question: Do you go to orchestral concerts for a refined cultural experience or because the conductor gets you hot? From a facsimile of a balcony seat at Northrop Auditorium, Mary Schweitzer sang: "I've this MAD, really BAD thing for Mr. Skrowaczewski." The maestro, by the way, continues to conduct in his nineties.

"You Gotta Have Hate" and "SuperpatrioticantiCatholicsegregation" (1965)

While the former borrowed a tune from *Damn Yankees* and the latter from *Mary Poppins*, they carried the right tone for *The First Annual Race Riot Revue*.

"Updale" and "The Pirates of Pennzoil" (1980)

The first a bluesy lament about the funky Uptown neighborhood taking on the trappings of a suburban shopping mall, the second a Gilbert and Sullivan–esque take on the Arab oil embargo that was causing gas lines and price hikes. Both are from *The Year the Grinch Stole the Election*.

"America, You'll Do" (1988)

This patriotic anthem about America the adequate was the finale of *Future Tense; or, Rubbered Bothered Baby Boomers* and was revived in several best-of revues.

"We're Leaving the Same Man Today" (1989)

In *Scared Shiftless*, Christine Decker and Michelle Cassioppi portrayed two bleach-blond country-western singers who chirped out this song, halting it periodically to cite Shakespeare, Euripides and Carl Jung to get to the heart of what women really want.

"Who Owns Me Now?" (1989)

In *Don't Worry, Be Stupid*, Peter Staloch and Peter Breitmayer delivered this vaudeville number sung by two corporate lackeys who consider three takeovers in twenty-four hours a slow day at the office.

"The Southern Fried Sisters of Song" (1992)

In the election-year extravaganza, *Mad in the USA; or Riot, You'll Like It*, those sisters were Hilary Clinton and Tipper Gore.

"The Ovarian Sisters" (1993)

In his review of *Better Than Sex*, the *Star Tribune*'s Peter Vaughan praised this angry pair of folk singers, saying, "Melissa Denton and Chris Kliesen Wehrman are deliciously deranged as these gaping, guitar-strumming wounds."

"Power" (1993)

Another tour de force for Chris Kliesen Wehrman, this one from *$pent Over Backwards; or, The All Fools Revue*. It was a lengthy cabaret song in the vein of Bertolt Brecht and Kurt Weill in which she portrayed the seductress and femme fatale of the title and sang of how she's been controlling things throughout human history.

"Teen Runaway" (1995)

Holiday…or Else featured Ahna Brandvik channeling the Virgin Mary as she belted out this old-fashioned greaser ballad (of the "Leader of the Pack" school) about two Nazareth teens in love and what happens when the Messiah makes three.

WHEN IT COMES TO LONGEVITY with the Brave New Workshop, music director Peter Guertin is the record holder, the length of his involvement in putting revues together surpassed only by Dudley Riggs himself. He was first hired for the touring company in April 1989 and worked with them and at ETC until he was "called up to the big leagues" and asked to be music director of Brave New Workshop in 1992. He was away from the company from 1995 to '98 but has been at the keyboard for almost every revue since. Here are some of his favorite songs from Brave New Workshop revues, with his comments:

"The Supreme Court Song" (1986)

"This song by Drew Jansen from *The Viceman Cometh* had everything going for it. The actors were dressed in Supreme Court robes, singing about what laws they were going to strike down. Abortion, women's rights, gay rights, et cetera. It had many different musical styles, such as madrigal and blues. Also, beautifully sung by the cast."

Minneapolis Star Tribune critic Mike Steele said:

> *You've got to love a show that begins with a chorus of boogying U.S. Supreme Court justices singing about saving us from ourselves. "We gave you freedom and you had fun," they twitter, "But you swung too far on the pendulum."…Sounding like a wing of the Meese commission on pornography—"Pictures of the human form/are deviations from the norm"—the justices finally raise their plaintive voices in a rhapsody of hope for the future, when babies will be born fully clothed.*

"The Cow Song" (1986)

"Written by Peter Staloch for *The Viceman Cometh*, this was sung by a cow on her way to slaughter. The costume consisted of horns and one hoof. I asked Peter why only one hoof, and he said that that was all the money in the show budget. Probably true. What I liked about this song was that it had a certain

Jacques Brel quality to it. It was a nice tango piece. The song actually made me question my meat eating habits. Beautiful and lyrically smart." Among the lyrics: "You don't like to meet the meat you eat."

"Fear Song" (1989)

"For *Scared Shiftless*, Drew Jansen wrote this nice, bluesy swing song that involved a woman imagining all her fears of the world. It was sung by a male trio, while she pantomimed. She was dressed in a white robe and part of it was performed under black light. The men had white gloves on and it looked like she was a marionette, dancing under their control. It reminded me of those old cartoons in the '30s! Brilliant lyrics and performance."

"Manic Depression" (1989)

Written by Steven Schaubel for *Don't Worry, Be Stupid*, "this was a sort of dreamy, slurry song. It was one guy on stage, Peter Breitmayer, singing about what it is like being manic depressive. I believe the opening line was: 'I'm hanging ten on a wave of manic depression.' Really meandering, dream-like melody. The big laugh was, during the blackout, before the song started, he hooked specially made boots to harnesses on the stage, which locked him in place. He was situated far down center. When he hit a certain part of the song, he would sway towards the audience and make them gasp. It was a beautiful sight gag that fit the song perfectly."

"Gay Guys (Scare the Hell Out of Me)" (1990)

This song was written by Steven Schaubel for *Censorship of Fools; or, Jesse at the Helm*. "A lone watchman in a museum filled with [Robert] Mapplethorpe [photography] and homoerotic statues. He's disgusted by the statues of two men and two women kissing. He sings this beautiful, bossa nova–style ballad about his disgust. The statues come to life and dance while he sings. He trades insults with them, but the final phrase of the song is 'We're all human,' sung in this beautiful harmony. Very, very touching, until the guard audibly cringes. A brilliant button to the song."

"The Phantom of the Election" (1992)

"Written by Jeff Goodson and myself for *Mad in the USA; or, Riot, You'll Like It*, this actually was a thirty-five- to forty-minute opera we wrote regarding the Clinton, Bush and Perot election campaign. It loosely followed the story of the original *Phantom of the Opera*. It had many great musical moments, including a damn fine ballad. The Phantom, as revealed at the end, is none

A tango twist emerges in 1988's *Safer Than Sex*. *Left to right*: Christine Decker, Gene Larche, Peter Staloch, Michelle Cassioppi and Jim Detmar.

other than Richard Nixon, trying for one last comeback. The audience loved it. What I love about it is the fact that Dudley actually let us consume the whole second act with wall-to-wall music. Dudley always loved and supported music in the shows. It was a gutsy and risky idea that really paid off. Not sure if we could ever do something like this again."

"The Ballad of Seamus O'Leary" (2001)
"Written by Caleb McEwen and myself for *How to Try in Business Without Really Succeeding*, this was an Irish ballad about a copy machine repairman. It was a wonderful story presented in the old Irish ways of story telling. It had a dance break in it that was like *Riverdance*. What else could you ask for?"

"The Vagina Song" (2001)
"Written by Katy McEwen and myself for *Sex in the Cities: The Edina Monologues*, it featured a nun explaining the do's and don'ts of the vagina. It had a Gilbert and Sullivan feel to it. The part of the song that people STILL talk about is the pirates who enter to sing the final chorus. Why? I don't know, but it made me laugh every single performance."

Dudley Riggs, pictured in 1988 at 2605 South Hennepin Avenue.

17

TOUCH ME AGAIN FOR THE VERY FIRST TIME; OR, THIS ELECTION IS RIGGSED

Delegating—that's what the founders of most successful businesses do more and more over time. They wean themselves away from the machinations of everyday operations and focus on the big-picture perspective, thinking more about long-range planning and legacy.

In a 1991 *Star Tribune* article by Peter Vaughan about the making of a typical Brave New Workshop show, director Mark Bergren said:

> *Right after one show is up, Dudley and I have a meeting and toss around some ideas for the next one. But Dudley leaves us alone. He has a lot of trust in us. He's involved in picking the theme and I touch base with him on our progress, but he allows us to develop the show.*

In the same article, Dudley describes himself as "a ghostly presence over the theater" who tries to walk a line between involvement and interference.

> *I do very little in the way of interfering with the flow of the script. I give them a pretty free hand except I keep nudging them. I do reserve the right to veto things, and I do on occasion, either because an idea or skit doesn't work or perhaps because it's too long and might be used in a future show...The biggest concern is to deal with something visible enough in the public eye, but not yet old hat.*

That story may have sold Dudley's contributions short for, by that time, he had returned to directing revues himself. He had co-directed *The Girth of a Nation; or, Alice Doesn't Work Out Here Anymore* with Jim Detmar in 1988 and then took the helm for 1989's *More Fun than Baseball; or, Field of Wet Dreams* and 1990's best-of revue *Touch Me Again (For the Very First Time)*. His real directorial renaissance was yet to come: between 1993 and '96, Dudley directed eight shows.

However, he suggests that he was doing some directing all along. He said:

> *I estimate no more than 10 out of 250 original productions were exclusively directed by a director that I had hired. Almost always, I was involved in shaping the shows and in trying to maintain my standards and what is now known as the Riggsian view. I was reluctant to give a totally free hand to others, as I wanted to maintain the standards I valued.*
>
> *For* What's So Funny About Being Female?…*I wanted to bring some production values and point of view to stand-up, which previously had been one person at a microphone followed by another person at the microphone followed by another, et cetera, a banal structure in my view. So I tried to bring a political point of view and some narrative to an evening of comedy that previously had seemed to me so segmented.*
>
> *The whole rash of shows* [I directed] *came about largely because I felt that we had gotten stuck in a presentation style that needed to reflect more on the wider point of view.*

Dudley also returned to commenting on local politics, as he and the company had in the early days. *More Fun than Baseball* cast a jaundiced eye toward the Minneapolis City Council. Melissa Denton reportedly did a great imitation of gregarious council member (and later radio host) Barbara Carlson, with Greg Triggs portraying paean of progressivism Brian Coyle and Mark Copenhaver as crusty old Northeaster Walt Dziedzic.

The *Star Tribune*'s Peter Vaughan called 1990's *Touch Me Again (For the Very First Time)*:

> *A fast-moving, often hilarious collage of skits drawn, for the most part, from previous Workshop shows.…Among the targets are American education, New Age zealots, the Minnesota lottery, poet Robert Bly, the male consciousness movement, corporate takeovers, telemarketing and death. This is the crème de la crème of recent Riggs revues, and it bubbles with wit and spontaneity under the crisp direction of Riggs himself.*

Among the highlights were Tom Winner as a man having a heart attack whose wasted life flashes before him and a principal excoriating parents for not doing their jobs.

Arguably the best review that Vaughan ever wrote of a Brave New Workshop show regarded 1990's *Censorship of Fools; or, Jesse at the Helm*. The show was largely inspired by South Carolina senator Jesse Helms's efforts to defund or eliminate the National Endowment for the Arts. Vaughan's review took the form of an open letter to Helms from one of his admirers, "a founding member of the Twin Cities chapter of the 4-F club (that's Freedom from Filth and Fornication)." Its "author" expressed shock and incredulity at such sketches as the "Planned Patriotism" clinic, the "Art Police" and "Porn Flakes," which its advertisement called "the breakfast cereal that doubles as sex education for the youngsters of the '90s. Porn Flakes is complete nutrition—including 12 assorted sex part shapes—and full of moral fiber."

Indeed, the company grew more political in the '90s. Evidence of this was in 1992's *The Recession Follies: BUSHwhacked*, featuring "The Kiwis of Wrath." In this sketch, John Steinbeck's Joad family piles into its aging Volvo. They leave decaying Silicon Valley to return to Oklahoma, stopping to put all of their cash into lottery tickets (seemingly their only possible escape from poverty). Their misadventures include encountering President George (H.W.) Bush betting the country's remaining cash at the craps table in an attempt to get the United States out of debt.

After the election of Bill Clinton in 1992, it wasn't long before the Workshop started seeing dire things on the horizon. Most troublingly, what seemed to be coming from the left was a new desire to regulate acceptable language. In a 1993 *Star Tribune* story about the subject, Dudley said, "I think we are in a book-burning time. It reminds me of any time when an oppressed people get a little power. They tend to abuse it, and we are seeing a lot of abuse of power right now."

Perhaps it was this fire in the belly about the current state of things that brought Dudley back to the director's chair with regularity. In 1994, he first directed *Victim Nation: The Don't Blame Me Review* and then *Without a Clue: The Dumbing of America*. Peter Vaughan wrote of *Victim Nation*:

> *Most of it is dead on as it exposes, both comically and painfully, what a bunch of whiners Americans have become. Whether accused of minor social infractions or murder, no one seems willing to take responsibility for his or her actions. With the eager assistance of therapists, sociologists and lawyers, malfeasants of all stripes bravely blame their crimes on their*

victims…And doctors come in for a few swipes in a rewritten Hippocratic Oath that astutely balances care and greed.

It seems a similar barbed tone held through that fall's *Without a Clue*, of which Vaughan wrote:

In the view of the Riggsians, we have become mental cripples, the limitless potential of our brains eroding hourly. We are sheep, eager to follow the dictates of others while lacking the intelligence and confidence to think for ourselves…It has a snappy skit about a monied middle-aged couple being appalled at the incursion of liberal arts and intellectualism into the life of their college-age son. Also hitting the mark was a fractured fairy tale from Oliver Stone…"The Four Selfish Bastard Pigs," which pinpoints some of the purveyors of our daily dose of dumb.

Dudley also directed 1995's *Virtual Reality Bytes: Lost on the Information Superhighway*, of which Vaughan wrote in his *Star Tribune* review, "This bright revue contrasts the dominance of the alleged labor-saving computer and the accompanying communications revolution with a nervous world in which meaningful communication is shrinking. It's funny and a bit sad." The troupe followed that with the Dudley-directed *No Newt is Good Newt: The 104th Congressional Follies*. That revue featured a mock game show in which contestants wagered social benefits like retirement, healthcare and education against the chance of sudden and unearned prosperity.

Among the shows he directed, Dudley confesses to a soft spot for his work with *What's So Funny About Being Female?* And, he said, "I always thought that *No Newt is Good Newt* was a politically effective show. Today, people still come up to me and quote some of the lines from that show."

Oh, and it was a rough holiday season in 1995–96 at the Brave New Workshop, as chronicled by this January of '96 item in the *Star Tribune*:

The jokesters at Dudley Riggs' Brave New Workshop are hoping for healthier times than dogged the recently closed Holiday…or Else *during its 12-week run…The illnesses that struck the cast and crew included pneumonia, pleurisy, high fevers, an extruded disk, bronchitis, concussion, arthritis, rashes, flu, damaged knee ligaments and tonsillitis. The problems resulted in two emergency room visits and one prolonged hospital stay that kept accompanist Peter Guertin out of the show for more than two weeks.*

When senator Jesse Helms went on the attack about what the National Endowment for the Arts was funding (partially based on an inaccurate secondhand account of a Minneapolis performance), the Brave New Workshop examined the issue in 1989's *Private Parts*. *Left to right*: Gene Larche, Peter Staloch and Peter Breitmayer.

Yet, with all the ailments, absenteeism among the actors was minimal. One actor missed one performance, another missed a couple.

Five pianists had to fill in for Guertin, as local professional musicians tend to get pretty booked around the holidays.

But 1996 was a banner year in that not only did Dudley direct three productions, but they also were used to comment on that year's presidential election. It has gone down in history as a comfortable runaway for incumbent Bill Clinton, but Dudley and company took aim at the sad predictability of the whole process in *Campaign in the Neck: This Election is Riggsed!* It employed a Greek chorus to give a sense of the inevitability of how things would unfold as the puppet of the fictional Recovery Party ran for president while surrounded by wheelers and dealers (one of whom sells his soul several times over).

In order to promote the show, Dudley announced that he was forming his own political party, the Brave New Party, and would be running for president on the ballot in Minnesota. Company members and others hit the streets to gather the two thousand signatures necessary. They didn't make it, but Dudley's name may have been among the 2,903 write-in votes cast in Minnesota that November 5.

This flurry of activity—taking charge of directing the revues, running for president—turned out to be the final surge in his thirty-nine years of heading the Brave New Workshop. Everything changed in February 1997.

Jenni Lilledahl and John Sweeney in the room full of posters from past shows at 2605 South Hennepin Avenue.

18

THE BALLAD OF JOHN AND JENNI; OR, A DEAL WITH DUDLEY

Y ou could call John Sweeney an escapee from the world of corporate finance. His energetic, gregarious manner and skill at cutting deals had made him successful in commercial real estate, and by his mid-twenties, he was the suit-clad co-founder of Brentwood Commercial and a marketing consultant for Keewaydin Real Estate Services. The descendant of Wisconsin dairy farmers was making more money than he ever imagined possible by this point in his life.

But it was a hectic existence, and he went looking for a release valve to let off some of the pressure. He found it in an improvisational comedy class at Stevie Ray's Comedy Cabaret in Minneapolis.

Jenni Lilledahl was from the Minneapolis suburb of Coon Rapids. Theater was among her studies at Augsburg College, a liberal arts school in Minneapolis's West Bank neighborhood, and after graduation, she found a job in communications. But she was also looking around for ways to scratch her theatrical itch and found it in a class at Stevie Ray's.

As Steve Rentfrow (better known as Stevie Ray) recalled:

> In 1991, Jenni began improv classes…and soon became one of our troupe members. In 1992, John Sweeney approached me for private training in stand-up. He soon joined improv classes and, when he worked his way up to the "Performance Level" class, met a single, attractive woman in class, Jenni Lilledahl. Since improv attracts a lot of single men, my partner Pamela Mayne and I wondered who would end up asking Jenni for a date. Little did we realize it would be John.

> *At the time, we had three improv troupes that would perform on their own nights…Each troupe had its own director, and Pamela directed the Monday night troupe, the Wizards of Odd. Every six months, we would re-audition from our entire school, and the three directors would haggle over who got which performer. When it came down to John Sweeney, the last spot, two of the directors didn't want him in their troupes because they thought he was too hard to handle. Pamela stepped up and said, "I'll take him!"*

By the fall of 1993, Sweeney had a job in the cast at the Brave New Workshop, making his debut in *Holiday on Nice: The Second Coming* and performing in all of the revues through early 1995.

Sweeney later told *Forbes* magazine:

> *I left my $100,000-a-year job to become a comedian, paid $200 a week. When I got my first big laugh, it was similar to the rush that I got when I made my first big sale, only better. I knew comedy was what I wanted to do for the rest of my life.*

Not long after he came on board, Sweeney started encouraging Dudley to have the company do more corporate training centered on improvisation. During the run of the 1994 holiday show, *Mix-Up in the Manger: Miracle on 26th Street*, Sweeney offhandedly said to Dudley that, if he were ever interested in selling the Brave New Workshop, he'd be interested in talking to him about it.

"I kept that in my mind," Dudley said.

A casting director encouraged Sweeney to check out the Chicago scene, so he relocated there in 1995 and started taking classes at the Second City and then landed a spot on its corporate touring company. A year later, Lilledahl joined that troupe, too. But it wasn't long before Dudley came calling.

Now sixty-four, Dudley had decided that this recent flurry of directing activity might be a fitting end to his career arc at the Brave New Workshop. He had remarried in 1988 and wanted to spend more time with his wife, University of Minnesota professor Pauline Boss. He also wanted to do more writing, encouraged by writing classes he took at Harvard University while his wife was on sabbatical there. So he called up Sweeney in Chicago and asked him if he'd like to buy the company.

First, Sweeney asked the folks at the Second City if they were interested in purchasing the Brave New Workshop, and he set up a meeting between Dudley and the folks there. But Dudley made clear that he wanted the company to remain the Brave New Workshop and not a Second City franchise, so he passed. So Sweeney assembled some financing, and they cut a deal. Demonstrating perhaps that Dudley had been doing the work of three people, the new co-owners would be Sweeney, Lilledahl and Mark Bergren. Sweeney would run the company and helm the corporate arm (and its customized workplace training and corporate entertainment). The artistic director of Brave New Workshop from 1985 to '94, Bergren would return to oversee the productions. Lilledahl would head up the company's classes and curricula.

The deal was announced on February 21, 1997, at a press conference at 2605 South Hennepin. Dudley started the event by taking the stage and improvising off the newspaper, as in the days of old, finally coming to the story he wanted to share about selling the company. The room was full of BNW alumni who told stories and gave Dudley a rousing and affectionate ovation. He fitted Sweeney and Lilledahl with new bow ties, which he regarded as the appropriate uniform for the position. Governor Arne Carlson declared it "Brave New Workshop Day" in Minnesota.

Sweeney and Lilledahl became partners in more than just business: they married in 1998 and now have two children.

Melissa Peterman made her Brave New Workshop debut in the 1997 revue, *Beanie Baby Barbecue; or, Something's Burning on the World Wide Weber.*

19

CRUISING, CALHOUN AND PLAYING THE PALACE; OR, THE HENNEPIN HOP

The first year the Workshop was under the leadership of Bergren, Lilledahl and Sweeney was a busy one. Old friends wished to become involved again, and a summer revue, *Beanie Baby Barbecue*, had quite a cast: Beth Gilleland and Dane Stauffer joined two holdovers from the last few years—Caleb McEwen and Joshua Will—and a newcomer to the troupe, the funny, flamboyant Melissa Peterman. Another alum from earlier years, Jay Reilly, directed. It was something of an intergenerational mix, but critics and audiences agreed that it worked.

Bergren had been working as a show director at Disney World in Orlando, Florida, for the past few years and that helped open the door for the first major new initiative under the new ownership. In August 1997, it was announced that Brave New Workshop would create the first improvisational comedy company at sea. It would have resident troupes on board two Disney cruise ships. The 2,600-passenger *Disney Magic* would set sail in the summer of 1998. The *Disney Wonder* would receive its champagne christening the following November. Each of the massive ships would have a nighttime entertainment district that included a 150-or-so-seat theater at which the Workshop would perform six shows a night. The maiden voyage was already sold out by August 1997.

The launch of the *Magic* was delayed, but a Brave New Workshop cast of eight—including Bergren, Peterman and Stauffer—headed to Italy in 1998 for a month of rehearsals before boarding for a three-week crossing to

The emergence of certain marital aids made for fine fodder for this 1998 poster.

Florida with stops in Portugal and the Bahamas along the way. A second cast would replace them after six months.

It was regarded as a big financial boon to the Brave New Workshop, which had been operating on a shoestring budget since its inception. But, while it boosted annual revenue by 105 percent, the costs involved meant that the company roughly broke even. While the on-board shows attracted good crowds, the people tended to stay in their seats and not order as much to drink as Disney would have liked. When the initial two-year contract was up, the revues were replaced by dueling pianists.

The cruise ships were a relatively low-risk proposition but such could not be said of another 1998 venture: the Brave New Workshop moved four blocks south to Calhoun Square, a shopping mall at the Uptown crossroads of Hennepin and Lake. This would require building a whole new theater space, albeit one with plenty of parking and nearby restaurants. The company put $400,000 into the project and expanded its staff to twelve full-time and fifteen part-time employees.

The new owners hoped that the move would double ticket sales, but they increased by only 6 percent over the course of three years. It was a difficult time for theaters everywhere, as the expansion of the Internet and increased video offerings led to more cocooning. Then came the terrorist attacks of September 11, 2001, which dampened spending habits. Now, what was imagined to be an upgrade in environs instead seemed to be a bad fit. Perhaps the Brave New Workshop's iconoclastic identity was partially tied up with being in that ragged little storefront on a far less chi-chi stretch of Hennepin. That's the venue to which the company returned in 2002.

As Sweeney told community newspaper the *Southwest Journal* in 2011, "After Calhoun Square, we were really, really, really screwed financially. We put all our eggs in that basket."

That said, Calhoun Square required taking a space in a relatively new mall (built in 1983) and turning it into a theater. Taking an old theater and making it usable for public performance is quite another task. The Brave New Workshop expanded eastward when it signed a lease and started to renovate the Palace Theater in downtown St. Paul, which had been known as the Orpheum in its cinema days from 1925 to '84. In the ornate lobby, the company presented long-running dinner shows like the audience-interactive *Flanagan's Wake* and *Minnesota: It's Not Just for Lutherans Anymore*. The capital city venture lasted three years, with the company departing in 2005.

What Brave New Workshop presents at Christmastime is usually a far cry from your typical *Christmas Carol* or *Nutcracker*, as evidenced by this 1999 poster.

So 2605 South Hennepin—which had always remained the venue for Brave New Institute classes and the company's administrative offices—was once again home to the Brave New Workshop's performances.

As for the ownership being a triumvirate, in 1999, Mark Bergren decided that he would like to pursue other things. Sweeney and Lilledahl bought out his share of Brave New Workshop and became sole owners.

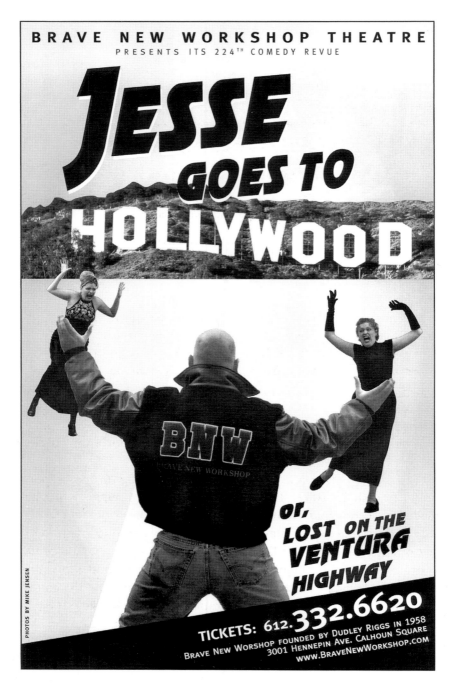

When Jesse Ventura was elected governor of Minnesota in 1998, it inspired this 1999 revue. (Left to right) Melissa Peterman and Shanan Wexler are held aloft by John Sweeney as the governor.

20

YOUR OFFICE COULD BE A COMEDY TROUPE; OR, A CUBICLE NAMED DESIRE

Audiences may not have been growing by that much, but the student body in the Brave New Workshop's educational arm certainly was. Lilledahl promoted the Brave New Institute at every opportunity, and the number of students grew from five in 1997 to over two hundred in 1999.

With Bergren gone, Sweeney took over directing duties for all of the Brave New Workshop revues at Calhoun Square from late 1999 through 2000. In 2002, he turned the artistic director mantle over to Caleb McEwen, who had been with the company since 1996, and set to looking for a way to create more revenue streams for the business.

He finally tapped into a relative gusher by beefing up the corporate training branch in 2002. The newly re-dubbed "Creative Outreach" provided speeches and training sessions that focused on increasing a workplace's productivity, innovation and creativity through learning the tenets of improvisation. The Brave New Workshop started taping comical corporate videos about common workplace problems and thinking on your feet. And word spread through executive suites around the country. Larger and more prominent corporations started booking Creative Outreach, and BNW started customizing presentations and breakout sessions to deal with specific challenges being faced by each company.

So Sweeney was able to fuse his two professional personas—the corporate real estate deal maker of his twenties and the creator of comedy since—and turn it into something lucrative for the Brave New Workshop.

Sweeney said in a 2011 *Southwest Journal* story:

> *At Brave New Workshop, coming up with a new idea for a show or for marketing is relatively risk-free and easy. And, once you come up with one, you'll be heralded and appreciated for the effort. Whereas once you get up to having 10,000 employees, there are about a million reasons employees are reluctant to come up with new ideas.*

His keynote speeches and workshops often concentrate on trying to break out of the "silo" mentality that can plague large workplaces, in which goals and tasks are overly compartmentalized and specialized and communication between departments stagnates. It's proven a message that corporate brass thinks worth hearing; by 2011, Sweeney's seminars and talks were being used by corporations like Microsoft and General Mills, and he'd written two books about improv as a tool in the workplace. Creative Outreach was now accounting for about two thirds of Brave New Workshop's $2 million in annual revenue, while ticket sales brought in about a quarter of it.

The cast of 2007's *YouCube: This Company Loves Misery. Left to right*: Mike Fotis, Ellie Hino, Joe Bozic, Josh Eakright and Lauren Anderson. *Collection of Joe Lampi.*

As Sweeney told the *Southwest Journal*:

> *It's odd, because it kind of started out of desperation, but the truth is I've grown very passionate about it. It seems really cool that this guy named Dudley Riggs started a theater in 1958 and introduced the Twin Cities to improv, and now, because of that, 3M is doing a better job, it's more fun to work at Best Buy, and people at Thrivent treat each other better.*

To underline the key points he's made in a corporate presentation, Sweeney eschews bullet points on a PowerPoint presentation in favor of having knives thrown at him. McEwen is part of a juggling and knife-throwing trio called the Danger Committee, which periodically presents late-night shows at the Brave New Workshop. At Creative Outreach presentations, Sweeney will stand in front of a board with words printed on it that he hopes will be the corporate audience's main takeaway ideas. McEwen will then throw knives into each of the words, zipping them by the edges of Sweeney's body. It certainly gets an audience's attention.

Katy and Caleb McEwen in a poster for a critically lauded two-person show from 2005.

21

THE ADVENTURES OF CALEB AND KATY; OR, DISCOUNT FAMILY VALUES

John Sweeney and Jenni Lilledahl weren't the only couple that kept the Workshop afloat during the first decade of the twenty-first century. When Sweeney turned the position of artistic director over to Caleb McEwen in 2002 ("I found out I was artistic director when someone pointed it out to me in the program," McEwen said), who knew that McEwen would direct twenty-nine revues by the end of the decade, appearing in eleven of them?

Four of those shows were co-directed by his wife, Katy McEwen. She acted in more productions than anyone else over the course of the decade. If that makes the Brave New Workshop sound like a mom-and-pop and mom-and-pop operation (they all became literal moms and pops during the decade, as well), it should be pointed out that the company had a solid core of writer/performers for much of the decade that included Mike Fotis, Lauren Anderson and Joe Bozic.

But every show involved one McEwen or the other or both, especially when the company stripped down for a show each year in the mid-'00s. In early 2003, McEwen called up a Chicago-based Workshop alum, Matt Craig, and asked him to create and perform a two-man show with him that became *Martha Stewart: Prison Vixen; or, It's a Good Thing*, which took aim at Americans' sense of entitlement. Then, it was Katy's turn in 2004, as she and Shanan Wexler (now Custer) developed their own two-hander called *Das Bootylicious; or, Women of Mass Destruction*.

Perhaps it was only a matter of time before Katy and Caleb ended up in their own two-person show, and it was one of the most acclaimed Brave New Workshop revues of this century (well, thus far, anyway). It was called *Shut Your American Pie-Hole; or, Discount Family Values*, and if you sense some hostility in the title, well, that's appropriate, for there was plenty expressed onstage. In his review of the 2005 show, Dominic Papatola of the *St. Paul Pioneer Press* called it:

> *Maybe the most cheesed-off comedy show I've ever seen. These two are angry—angry at the hypocrisy, angry at shallow-mindedness, angry at jingoism and timidity and racism disguised as patriotism. And so the husband-and-wife team has checked subtlety and good taste at the door, launching a take-no-prisoners humor offensive. This is hard-edged, brilliant comedy, the kind of fearless satire that makes satire worth seeing.*

In its spring 2006 "Best of the Twin Cities" issue, alternative weekly *City Pages* named the show Best Comedy in its local theatrical roundup. It also picked up on the surliness, saying:

> *There has been a distinct and appealing vibe of crankiness emanating from the Brave New Workshop of late, and no show better captured that foul mood than this one…Caleb's pissed-off braininess worked to great effect with Katy's poison wholesomeness…The final portions crossed into greatness, with…the very notion of the American family being held up for scorn. It was a beautiful night.*

It would be nice to say that Caleb and Katy McEwen arrived at the Brave New Workshop as a package deal, but they actually came separately. They moved to the Twin Cities in 1995 after graduating from Ohio's Wright State University, and by the following year, both had been offered jobs at both the Brave New Workshop and the Children's Theatre Company. "We decided it would be best to divide and conquer," Caleb said, "so I went to the BNW, and Katy went to the CTC." While at Children's Theatre Company, Katy said that she had a strong mentor in veteran actor Wendy Lehr. "I thought my entire career would be as her understudy," she told the *Star Tribune* in 2004. "I learned that comedy is so specific and calculated."

The company responded to media coverage of Hurricane Katrina with 2006's *Saturday Night FEMA; or, The Roof, the Roof, the Roof is Under Water! Left to right*: Mike Fotis, Joe Bozic, Katy McEwen and Lauren Anderson.

In 1999, Katy did her first Brave New Workshop show and has been there ever since, now serving as associate artistic director after a stint as co-artistic director with Caleb for a few years.

If anyone felt that the Brave New Workshop had lost its bite, it came roaring back with McEwen and McEwen on board. The U.S. government's response to Hurricane Katrina (and the media's coverage of it) got it with both barrels in 2006's *Saturday Night FEMA; or, The Roof, the Roof, the Roof is Under Water!* You can bet that all that the company was learning about the inner workings of corporations from its Creative Outreach work came into play in creating *YouCube; or, This Company Loves Misery.* At that show's fictional conglomerate, OmnipoCorp, employees who showed initiative by suggesting creative ideas were rewarded by being allowed to shoot a hated mid-level executive.

Speaking of shooting, 2006's three-man show, *See Dick Shoot (And Other Signs of the Apocalypse),* had one of the sillier recurring bits of the decade, the cast responding to the new film *Snakes on a Plane* by offering live-action trailers for "Panthers in a Hovercraft," "Ferret in a Bobsled" and "Bear on a Ski Lift."

By decade's end, Caleb and Katy were co-directing a pair of *How to Make Love Like a Minnesotan* shows bearing the subtitles *Sleepless in Shakopee* and *Love Is in Bloomington*. Quinton Skinner of *City Pages* wrote:

> *Directors Katy and Caleb McEwen have steered this work exclusively into the realm of how men and women obsess over, love, endure, tire of, rediscover, take for granted, and generally co-exist with one another. It's no warm and fuzzy affair, but by the end, there's a welcome nod at the big picture, courtesy of Mike Fotis's final line. We walk into the night reminded that all things pass, that love is indeed the answer, and that we remain deeply ridiculous creatures.*

When asked to cite some of his favorite shows from his time at the Workshop, Caleb McEwen mentioned these:

> Sex in the Cities: The Edina Monologues *(2001) was a beautiful show. Everything about it worked—the sketches, the transitions, the set…Everything hit from beginning to end, and it had the longest single laugh in it that I've ever seen on our stage. Katy would get it each night doing a scene where she and Jim Robinson were a couple arguing while on home exercise equipment, and she would check her pulse after insulting him…This was the show playing during 9/11. We cancelled one performance because some of the performers were trapped out of town due to planes being grounded.*
>
> BUSHwhacked II: One Nation Under Stress *(2002) was our first original show back at 2605 after Calhoun Square. It was a look at the nation's reaction to 9/11, and looking back, it was very prescient. Audiences found it cathartic…The show would start with an actor on stage asking an audience member the date of their birthday. We would write the date in chalk on the theater wall and explain that Americans had become traumatized from the repetition of the phrase, "September 11th," so we were replacing the phrase "September 11th" with this audience member's birthday for the duration of the show to ease the tension and allow people to relax.*

Katy McEwen said of that show, "A lot of audience members had no interest in 'unpacking' that particular event at that time. But we thought it was important to look at it and move forward. I'm very proud of the theater for that choice."

Yet Caleb spoke of one show as ranking at the top for him.

> *My favorite show of all time was* Total Recall II: The Governator *(2003). On the surface, it was about the recall of Gray Davis in 2003, but from our standpoint, it was about using fear to achieve political goals…It was a very complicated plot of political machinations revolving around Arnold Schwarzenegger as an actual cyborg sent back from the future to take over the governorship of California. It involved time travel paradoxes, Machiavellian intrigue, media gamesmanship and a lot of other elements…Roughly the last twenty minutes of the show take place in complete darkness. This allowed us to have more than a dozen characters on stage played by the five actors…That show had several of the greatest theatrical moments I've ever been a part of.*
>
> *I also loved the device in* Spilling Me Softly; or, When the Gulf Goes Black, It Never Goes Back *(2010) where we parodied* Inception *by doing sketches within sketches within sketches within the mind of a Mexican immigrant who was being used to replace one of the actors for less pay.*
>
> *And* Fifty Shades of Gravy *(2015) is one of my favorites in recent memory.*

The latter show demonstrated that the Brave New Workshop hasn't lost its edge in dealing with race relations in America. Particularly memorable is a scene in which two clownish candidates for a firefighter job—virtually identical in attire, education, experience and demeanor—produce radically different reactions in one of the interviewers, who finds the African American candidate "thuggish." Andy Hilbrands goes on to deliver an insightful song about common terms that are used to point up racial differences in coded fashion.

So what makes Katy most proud from her Brave New Workshop tenure?

> *For me, personally, what I remember the most is creating great content for women, although we didn't really think of it that way. I didn't set out to make a feminist statement; I just wanted to create good work that was meaningful and fun. I didn't think, "I need to write strong female characters." I thought, "This is hilarious. I wrote it, and I want to be the one who gets to perform it." And my experience at the Workshop has always been that good work gets in the shows. So I made sure my work was good enough to get in. And I wasn't alone. Shanan Custer, Lauren*

Anderson, Ellie Hino—all women with unique voices creating great work that stood alone as "great work" not "great work for women." That is pretty cool, I think.

One of the company's most successful election shows was *The Lion, the Witch and the War Hero; or, Is McCain Able?* (2008). It also took that Best Comedy honor in *City Pages'* "Best of the Twin Cities." Cast member Josh Eakright remembered it as a show that would change week to week depending on what was happening in the presidential campaign. Eakright said:

That was such a great time for satire and an exciting time in our country. It brought us Sarah Palin, who made every weekend of shows feel like Christmas. There was always new material to insert, the news segments wrote themselves, and we had a slot where we got to write and perform new sketches until the next thing would happen and we'd replace it. Ellie Hino played a spot-on Palin and [Congresswoman Michele] *Bachmann, and Lauren Anderson wore a combed-over bald cap to play McCain after the debate where he wandered, seemingly*

Early in the 2008 presidential campaign, the Republicans had settled on John McCain while the Democratic race remained competitive, as communicated in this promotional image for *The Lion, the Witch and the War Hero. Left to right:* Josh Eakright, Lauren Anderson, Mike Fotis, Ellie Hino, Joe Bozic and Bobby Gardner. *Collection of Joe Lampi.*

lost. Also, I got to play Al Franken in a scene where I debated Norm Coleman [Bobby Gardner] *and ultimately wrestled Jesse Ventura* [Mike Fotis in a boa], *finishing him with a devastating diving double axe handle smash off the top rope.*

Of course, the Brave New Workshop alum emerged triumphant in both the ring and the election.

Caleb also spearheaded another project of note. With Dane Stauffer and John Sweeney, he wrote a play about the life and work of Dudley called *Dudley: Rigged for Laughter* that premiered at the History Theatre in St. Paul in 2010.

In 2011, Brave New Workshop moved to its new home at 824 Hennepin Avenue in downtown Minneapolis.

22

MIRACLE AT 824 HENNEPIN AVENUE; OR, UPTOWN, DOWNTOWN

If Minneapolis has a Main Street, it's Hennepin Avenue. It's the only major thoroughfare that runs through at least five distinctly different neighborhoods and is also a downtown destination for patrons of hotels, theaters, restaurants and bars. This is the street where the Brave New Workshop has always had a home base.

In July 2010, the city of Minneapolis put out the word about an available downtown space and asked for proposals about what to do with it. The address? 824 Hennepin Avenue.

It was most recently called Hennepin Stages, but prior to that had been Hey City Theater, so named for theatrical impresario Sandy Hey, who had directed revues at ETC in the late '80s and early '90s. It had a theater space upstairs but also a ground floor ballroom that came into much use during the interactive theater piece, *Tony 'n' Tina's Wedding*, that ran there from 1999 to 2004. Since then, the Hennepin Theatre Trust—owners and operators of the nearby Orpheum, State and Pantages theaters—had been presenting productions there, but the space wasn't really reestablishing an identity.

The old real estate man Sweeney saw immediate possibilities in it. The upstairs theater could be a more posh and symmetrical version of the space at 2605 Hennepin, while the main floor ballroom could be a long-needed venue for Creative Outreach presentations, allowing workers to get out of their home offices and, ideally, out of their ruts. The dressing rooms and rehearsal spaces wouldn't be nearly as cramped.

On opening night in 2011, the mayor of Minneapolis, R.T. Rybak, became involved in a sketch outside the theater that landed him atop an exercise bike.

After financing was secured, the sale was sealed on April 29, 2011, and renovations began. After christening the space in October with performances of the Dudley bio that had been premiered at History Theatre, *Dudley: Rigged for Laughter*, the official opening was on November 4, with plenty of coverage from local TV and papers and a red-carpet ceremony under the bright new neon-covered marquee that hung over the sidewalk on Hennepin. Dudley was present—as he had been for almost every opening night since he'd sold the theater—and he did his best to teach Sweeney how to tie a bow tie before the festivities began. Minneapolis mayor R.T. Rybak ended up riding an exercise bicycle on the red carpet to supposedly generate the juice needed to light the new marquee.

Another significant improvement over 2605: instead of just two restrooms that could each be used by one patron at a time—the ones that Pat Proft and Peter Tolan had cleaned as part of their duties back in the day—there were now multi-stall lavatories on two floors. Also on multiple levels were bars with full liquor licenses (as opposed to the wine and beer served at 2605), creating a new revenue stream that would prove quite lucrative. By 2015, liquor sales would account for over 15 percent of the Brave New Workshop's gross revenues.

Yes, it was only early November, but the space was christened with a holiday revue, *Miracle at 824 Hennepin Avenue; or, Skyway to the Manger Zone.*

Lauren Anderson engages the audience in the 2012 show *50 Shades of White: A Minnesota XXXmas*.

While securing the venue might not have exactly been a miracle but more a serendipitous fit, this had all the earmarks of the Minneapolis theater scene's rebel stepchild being now fully embraced as part of the local culture it had been lampooning for half a century. It felt kind of like the Rolling Stones being knighted or Al Franken being elected to the U.S. Senate.

So what would keep this from being "Calhoun Square, the Sequel?" Well, for one thing, Creative Outreach was now tremendously successful, so Brave New Workshop wasn't the hand-to-mouth venture it had been for so long. There would also be a fair amount of income from renting out the space to corporate clients. Lest this all seem a fantasy, you should know that it seems to have come true. During its fiscal year of 2014–15, Brave New Workshop pulled in about $3.1 million in gross revenues, 39 percent of it from Creative Outreach and about 24 percent from ticket sales. Tickets are moving well. The 2014 holiday show, *Twerking Around the Christmas Tree*, was the company's most popular production of this century.

As for the educational arm—now called "the Brave New Workshop Student Union"—it's doing just fine, serving a multi-generational student body of about 250 and acting as something of a farm system akin to what the Monday Night Company and the touring company used to be. It also

While Brave New Workshop's performances and many of its corporate events take place at 824 Hennepin Avenue, its school and corporate headquarters are now housed in this building a block away at 727 Hennepin Avenue, purchased in 2014.

has a new home of its own, also on Hennepin Avenue. In August 2014, Sweeney and Lilledahl bought a building a block down from the theater (727 Hennepin Avenue) and have renovated it into the home for the Brave New Workshop's corporate offices and school. When told of the planned purchase, Dudley Riggs remarked that he had looked at buying that very space decades ago.

Lady Liberty has long been a part of Brave New Workshop's branding, as have elements of the stars and stripes of the American flag.

The Brave New Workshop sign that hung above the door of 207 East Hennepin Avenue in the early '60s can still be found on the wall in the lobby at 824 Hennepin Avenue.

The building at 727 Hennepin will double as something of a museum where one can get a sense of the company's history through displays. Some of the old seats from 2605 are used in the new building's café and lounge areas.

But many of the most iconic artifacts can be found at 824 Hennepin. There's that "Satire!" sign that Richard Guindon painted in 1961, and Bud Lilledahl (Jenni's father) painted a new version of the lounging, cigar-puffing Miss Liberty (wearing Uncle Sam's pants) that has been gracing BNW dispatches and walls since the '60s. Dudley is on prominent display, too, thanks to a large portrait near the theater entrance.

As you enter the upstairs theater space where the Brave New Workshop revues are performed, you can look up and see a sign that dates to the early '60s with suns in the spaces between the words, "Brave New Workshop." Above and below it are words that have summed up the troupe's mission ever since that late-night brainstorming session in 1961: "Promiscuous Hostility, Positive Neutrality."

AFTERWORD

A nd now, through the magic of make-believe, lies, deception and deceit, and through the courtesy of the First, Second and Fourth Amendments…the Brave New Workshop!"

After completing his monologue and folding his newspaper under his arm, that's how Dudley Riggs would introduce the revues of the company's early years. Invoking the U.S. Constitution in his introduction was but one example of how, from the very beginning, Dudley and the Workshop would assert the American-ness of their mission. It came through in the theater company's signage, from that very first red, white and blue "Satire!" poster to the Stars and Stripes that covered its Uptown façade and the bedraggled Lady Liberty/Uncle Sam hybrid in its longtime logo.

Of course, satire is not a uniquely American art form. It has probably been around since some early human asserted control and was subjected to mockery, but it is an essential element to any free and open society, and one worth treasuring in a time when you don't hear the phrase, "I may not agree with what you say, but I'll defend to the death your right to say it," nearly as much as you once did or should.

Brave New Workshop should be saluted for its courage. Threats, harassment and vandalism have often come the company's way when it has criticized revered institutions. There have been death threats as recently as the past decade after it has slaughtered sacred cows onstage.

Clearly, some see satire as dangerous, as evidenced by the massacre of staff members at the Paris satirical paper *Charlie Hebdo*. But fear is a far more

Richard Guindon's hand-painted sign that graced the exterior of both 207 East Hennepin Avenue and 2605 South Hennepin Avenue can now be found in the lobby at 824 Hennepin Avenue.

serious threat to our species, especially if it keeps us from calling out the powerful for actions we see as abusive or unjust. And wrapping criticism in comedy has always been a fine way to serve up that spoonful of sugar that helps the medicine go down.

So rage on fearlessly, Brave New Workshop! You're at your best when you're most audacious. And you might be more important now than you've ever been.

DISTINGUISHED ALUMNI

H ere is but a small sampling of the many Brave New Workshop creators of comedy who have graced its stage since 1961:

Louie Anderson is a stand-up comedian, comic actor and an Emmy-winning creator of the series *Life with Louie*. He was the star of *The Louie Show* and host of *Family Feud*.

Michael Anthony was the longtime classical music critic for the *Star Tribune* in Minneapolis.

Jeff Cesario is an Emmy-winning writer and producer for *Dennis Miller Live* and *The Larry Sanders Show*.

Mo Collins is an actor best known for her six seasons on the Fox sketch comedy TV series *MadTV*.

Tom Davis was one of the original writers and performers on NBC's *Saturday Night Live*, as well as a writer for film and television. He died in 2012.

Richard Engquist was a musical theater lyricist best known for *Kuni-Leml* and *Little Ham*. He died in 2010.

Ed Flanders was an actor best known for his role on TV's *St. Elsewhere*. He died in 1995.

Al Franken was one of the original writers and performers on NBC's *Saturday Night Live*, a screenwriter, a host on Air America Radio, a bestselling author and a U.S. senator from Minnesota.

Jeff Gadbois is a successful voice actor whose dulcet tones have been heard in thousands of radio and television commercials.

A typically enthusiastic audience for 2012's *50 Shades of White*.

Richard Guindon made light of Minnesota culture in his cartoons for the *Minneapolis Tribune* until 1981 before disembarking for Detroit and doing the same for Michigan culture for the *Detroit Free Press* until 2006.

Jim Hudson is a character actor best known for his roles in *Die Hard 2*, *Joe Versus the Volcano* and *Bachelor Party*.

Peggy Knapp was co-host of the TV series *Newton's Apple* and *Hometime*.

Lorna Landvik is the author of several novels, including the bestsellers *Patty Jane's House of Curl*, *Angry Housewives Eating Bon Bons* and *The View from Mount Joy*.

Irv Letofsky was a longtime entertainment editor for the *Los Angeles Times*. He died in 2007.

Carl Lumbly is an actor best known for his regular roles on the TV series *Cagney and Lacey* and *Alias*.

Clark MacGregor became chairman of Richard Nixon's Committee to Reelect the President a month after the Watergate break-in.

Peter MacNicol had lead roles in the films *Dragonslayer* and *Sophie's Choice* and was a regular on the TV series *Chicago Hope*, *Ally McBeal* (for which he won an Emmy) and *Numb3rs*.

Michael McManus is an actor best known for his roles in the film *Poltergeist*, TV's *Lewis & Clark* and in multiple TV series guest spots.

Paul Menzel founded the Comedy Workshop in Houston, Texas, in 1977, teaching many of the improvisational methods he used during his years as artistic director of Brave New Workshop. Among the

Dudley Riggs and his wife, Pauline Boss, join the "protesters" outside the theater on opening night of *Occupy Arden Hills; or, Brother Can You Spare a Dome?* in 2012.

alumni of his Workshop are Bill Hicks, Sam Kinison, Brett Butler and Janeane Garofalo.

Melissa Peterman is best known for her role on TV's *Reba* but has also been a regular on *Baby Daddy* and host of *The Singing Bee*.

Pat Proft is a screenwriter who has written or co-written films in the *Naked Gun*, *Hot Shots*, *Police Academy* and *Scary Movie* series.

Dudley Riggs is a writer who continues to advise and support the owners of the Brave New Workshop.

Ann Ryerson is an actor best known for her role on the TV series *Curb Your Enthusiasm*.

Sue Scott has been a member of the cast of the American Public Media radio show *A Prairie Home Companion* since 1992.

Tom Sherohman was the screenwriter for the films *Modern Problems* and *Mr. Magoo*.

Rich Sommer is best known for his role on the TV series *Mad Men*.

Dane Stauffer remains an active performer on the Twin Cities theater scene.

Nancy Steen was a screenwriter for the TV shows *Happy Days*, *Night Court* and *Caroline in the City* and a producer for *Roseanne*.

Dan Sullivan was a theater critic for the *New York Times* and *Los Angeles Times* and is now a journalism professor at the University of Minnesota.

Faith Sullivan met Dan Sullivan while writing and performing at Brave New Workshop, and they had their wedding reception there. She is a successful novelist best known for *The Cape Ann* and *The Empress of One*.

Peter Tolan is an Emmy-winning writer for the TV series *Murphy Brown*, *Home Improvement* and *Rescue Me* and screenwriter for the films *Analyze This* and *Analyze That*.

Linda Wallem was a writer and producer for the TV series *Cybill, That '70s Show* and *Nurse Jackie*.

Lizz Winstead is a comedian who was co-creator and head writer of TV's *The Daily Show*.

Cedric Yarbrough is a comedian and actor best known for his roles on TV's *Reno 911!* and *The Boondocks*.

INDEX

Index

ABOUT THE AUTHOR

Despite Dudley Riggs once saying that "St. Paul doesn't really exist. It was made up by F. Scott Fitzgerald," Rob Hubbard has lived there all his life. The former artistic director of a small but award-winning Minneapolis theater company, he has spent most of the past few decades as a journalist, chiefly focusing on music, theater and the arts. The vast majority of his writing has appeared in the *St. Paul Pioneer Press*, but he's also been the editor and head writer for American Public Media's *Performance Today*.